BUSINESS INVESTIGATED

BUSINESS INVESTIGATED

Data and Issues in Business Studies, A Level and BTEC

Michael Watts and Matthew Glew

CollinsEducational
An imprint of HarperCollins*Publishers*

Published by **Collins Educational**,
77–85 Fulham Palace Road, Hammersmith, London W6 8JB
10 East 53rd Street, New York, NY 10022, USA

First published in 1992

ISBN 0 00 327483 7

British Library Cataloguing in Publication Data
A catalogue record for this book is available on request from the British Library.

Library of Congress Cataloging in Publication Data
A catalog record for this book is available on request from the Library of Congress.

Typeset in 9½ on 10 point Paladium by Burns and Smith Ltd, Derby
and printed in Great Britain by Scotprint Ltd., Musselburgh, Scotland

Contents

Introduction

Part A Businesses and Organizations

1 A Body Shop franchise 2
2 Small firms 4
3 Toyota – local production 6
4 British Rail 8
5 Virgin – growth through diversification 10

Part B People in Organizations

6 Training for the future 14
7 Fixing a deal at Finewood 17
8 Working for the Japanese 18

Part C Market Matters

9 The newspapers and magazine market 21
10 The market for sports and leisure footwear 24
11 The housing market 27
12 Filofax 30
13 Launching a new product 32

Part D Managing Business Performance

14 Marks and Spencer – financial performance 34
15 The Cromwell 36
16 Computers in manufacturing 38

Part E The impact of the wider business environment on the organization

17 Monica Davies and the Wilburyshire Ambulance Service – a case for the industrial tribunal 40
18 Industry and the environment 44
19 Government and small firms 48
20 The Budget 52
21 International competitiveness and the exchange rate 56
22 The effects of deflationary policies 60
23 Relocation 66
24 The Monopolies and Mergers Commission Report on the supply of beer, March 1989 70

Part F The integrated nature of business decisions

25 The growth of Ratners 74
26 MFI and the household furniture market 79

Introduction

AIMS

The book is designed to help students relate business studies to real-world situations, thus stimulating their interest in the subject and encouraging them to look beyond the immediate confines of the syllabus. In so doing it will help students to develop greater confidence and the appropriate skills in dealing with various aspects of business as required by A level and BTEC examinations in business studies. The units are designed to develop particular skills relating to the use of business terms; presenting, interpreting and evaluating business data; identifying business problems and opportunities; generating a range of solutions; evaluating alternatives; designing suitable strategies and supporting a case.

The presentation and approach of the book are designed to make it readily accessible to students who have experienced a GCSE approach to teaching and learning.

USING THE BOOK

The book is designed to complement, and to be used in conjunction with, a core business studies textbook. It is divided into a number of self-contained units. However it is not intended to be a systematic teaching package that must be worked through from beginning to end. Students may attempt units at whatever time seems appropriate during their studies. Teachers and students can, of course, be selective not only in the order in which they undertake units, but also in the way in which they approach the activities within each unit.

STIMULUS MATERIAL

The stimulus items have been chosen with several criteria in mind. They have been selected from both primary and secondary sources to reflect the type of business information that students are likely to meet both in examinations and assignments as well as their future business careers. In addition, they reflect many different methods of presentation and media sources. Finally, they have been chosen to present lively and interesting perspectives on the business issues under consideration.

UNIT ACTIVITIES

- The Investigation of Business Terms sections are intended to extend the student's business vocabulary and knowledge of business terms. They have been used in those units where it is felt to be necessary to help the student to understand the stimulus material.
- Short-Answer Questions are to help to develop the ability of factual recall, some degree of comprehension and application.
- The activities associated with Analysing Business Situations are intended to develop the skills of analysis, synthesis and evaluation. They also involve business decision-making and problem-solving skills and reflect the integrated nature of so many of these situations.

Some essay-style questions, including some drawn from past A level papers, have been included to provide examination practice.

The investigative analysis used in some units is intended to extend the student's awareness of secondary and primary sources of business information and how it may be collected, processed, interpreted and analysed.

The case studies provide a vehicle for the wider application of business skills and analysis of business situations.

The local studies reflect the particular requirements of the Cambridge Board, while also providing the context for BTEC assignments.

The role-play activities provide realistic simulations which help to develop oral communication skills and the ability to appreciate the wider aspects of business decision-making.

A Body Shop franchise

Figure 1.1

The BODY SHOP

Skin & Hair Care Preparations

Figure 1.2

UK FRANCHISE INFORMATION SHEET

The Body Shop currently has over 140 shops in the UK and more than 320 overseas, and we plan to continue growing throughout the 1990s by continuing to achieve high standards of retailing.

Our values have not changed since the first Body Shop was opened in 1976 in Brighton. Anita and Gordon Roddick are still the driving force behind the company, and our skin and hair care products are still produced from natural ingredients which are not tested on animals.

Our values are not just skin deep. We are totally committed to and involved with the communities in which we trade; from our head office based in Littlehampton, to the shop floor in many towns all over the world, to the Third World countries which supply many of our raw ingredients.

The Body Shop is a successful trader; it is also a force for social change. We are committed to further growth and success, to open more Body Shops in more places, to serve more people. To do this, we need committed franchisees who share our philosophies and are committed to promote actively our ideals, especially with regard to our staff and environmental issues. We look for franchisees who want to be actively involved in the business and who can confidently subscribe to the principle of 'profit with responsibility'. Most importantly, we are looking for people who can combine these elements with a sense of fun for everyone involved.

If you want to be a part of our family the attached information sheet outlines the basic facts of franchising with Body Shop, and tells you what to do next.

Figure 1.3

UK FRANCHISE PACK

THE FRANCHISE

A franchise shop is independently owned and run by the franchisee. The relationship between The Body Shop International and its franchisees is governed by a legal agreement which is renewable after five years. The agreement assures maximum autonomy for franchisees whilst maintaining The Body Shop's successful trading formula and its high standards. Over 70% of the UK's Body Shops are franchised.

THE FRANCHISEE

Franchisees are sincere, committed individuals (or partnerships) who share our business ethics and advance the aims of The Body Shop as a values-led company. Prospective franchisees must be prepared to work hard and should intend to work in their shop on a full-time basis. Ideally the franchisee should live in the community in which the shop is located.

THE COST

Current set-up costs in the UK are running at about £200,000 (March 1990). This includes shop fitting, design and legal fees, but excludes any lease premium, should it apply. Other financial data and advice are available at a later stage in the selection process.

THE LOCATION

You stand a better chance of selection if you are flexible in your choice of location. Our expansion is determined by the properties available. There is no need to look for a property yourself – our agents are constantly seeking suitable sites.

THE COMPETITION

We receive around 10,000 franchise applications per year and the competition is tough so it may mean a long wait.

THE NEXT STEP

If you are still interested in applying for a Body Shop franchise, write to the UK Franchise Department at:
The Body Shop International PLC, Hawthorn Road, Wick, Littlehampton, West Sussex BN17 7LR

Tell us briefly:
- about yourself.
- the areas in which you would like to operate.
- why you would like to own a Body Shop.

WE LOOK FORWARD TO HEARING FROM YOU.

Figure 1.4

Body Shop feels squeeze . . . or why other retailers are no longer green with envy

Ben Laurance

BODY SHOP, the trendy cosmetics retailer which wears its ecological conscience on its sleeve and its concern for animal welfare on its T-shirts, is finally feeling the effect of the squeeze on consumer spending.

The company, led by Anita Roddick, yesterday unveiled a respectable 29 per cent profits increase for the year to the end of February and boasted that the underlying growth in sales at its shops was 10 per cent over the year.

But it admitted that, since the beginning of this year, like-for-like sales growth had ground to a halt. Sales were flat in the first three months of 1990. Since April, turnover has been 7 per cent ahead – but only because Body Shop has pushed through price increases – a far cry from the picture two years ago, when the company's outlets were showing sales rises of around 30 per cent as they cashed in on the increasing preference for goods which proclaimed their greenness.

'There is a tendency in the market to believe that Body Shop can walk on water,' said retailing analyst Paul Deacon at Goldman Sachs. 'But experience in the 1980s should have taught people that no retailer can do that.'

Pre-tax profits were £14.5 million on turnover up by more than half at £84.5 million.

Of Body Shop's 450-plus outlets, about 90 per cent are franchised. The company now operates in 37 countries. It aims to break even in the US by the end of this year and has teamed with Japanese supermarket group, Jusco, to open outlets in Japan from October. By franchising, Body Shop has avoided the burdensome debt which has crippled other niche retailers such as Sock Shop.

But Body Shop is, nevertheless, asking investors for £30 million by selling new shares. The money will help fund planned capital spending of £50 million over the next three years. Some of the cash will go on new office buildings, a new research and development facility and a plant to make plastic bottles, now bought in from outside.

'Although the rate of sales growth has fallen right back, there is still plenty of untapped demand for the idea in Britain and overseas,' said Mr Deacon. Analysts are looking for profits of around £22 million in the current year to February. But the halt in underlying sales volume growth may force the stock market to think again about the rating of Body Shop shares – which are rated twice as highly as those of many other retailers.

(*Guardian*, 7 June 1990)

INVESTIGATION OF BUSINESS TERMS

Franchise. A contractual licence granted by the franchisor to the franchisee. The licence is normally purchased for an initial franchise fee with or without future royalty payments. The franchisee then receives a complete business package from the franchisor, including expertise and market research, financial planning, training, and use of the corporate name and its promotion through advertising. This allows the franchisee to operate his/her business to the same standards and format as all the other units in the franchised chain.

Values-led company. An organization which is in business not just to maximize profits but also to uphold certain business ethics and to fulfil wider economic, social, environmental or political objectives.

Niche retailers. A retailer stocking and selling a highly specialized range of products.

Untapped demand. Potential consumers who have not as yet come forward to purchase the good or service. This could be due to lack of awareness of the actual existence or the qualities of the product or service.

SHORT-ANSWER QUESTIONS

1. What is the basis of the relationship between the Body Shop International and its franchisees?
2. List four qualities that the Body Shop is looking for in its potential franchisees.
3. Explain the underlying principles behind the Body Shop's 'profit with responsibility'.
4. Why is the Body Shop more likely to be able to achieve its objectives if it selects the sites for the franchised shops?
5. Explain how the Body Shop has been feeling the squeeze on consumer spending.
6. Why has the Body Shop been able to continue to expand even when other retailers have been standing still?
7. Give two examples of vertical integration undertaken by the Body Shop.

ANALYSING BUSINESS SITUATIONS

1. Why do business organizations which have entered into a franchise arrangement generally have a higher success rate than those which try and develop their own business ideas from scratch?
2. To what extent have the fortunes of the Body Shop operation tended to mirror the values of society and the state of the economy?
3. From the beginning of 1990 the Body Shop's sales growth ground to a halt although between April and June 1990 its turnover increased by 7 per cent. Explain how this increase was brought about.
4. Suggest what might have been the commercial strategy behind the Body Shop's expansion abroad into 37 different countries.

ACTIVITIES

LOCAL STUDY

Assume that you have recently been made redundant as a buyer for a national chain of chemists' shops. Your total redundancy package is worth approximately £38,000. You have a four-bedroomed detached house with a market value of £150,000 and £30,000 outstanding on the mortgage. You have £21,000 in savings in the local Building Society and a strong desire to go into business on your own account.

On receiving the information shown as Figures 1.2 and 1.3 you decide to write to the Body Shop giving them the details they require. Draft a suitable letter making an application for a franchise which relates to your local area and reflects the financial circumstances outlined above. In the letter you should indicate how you intend to raise the £200,000.

ESSAYS

1. Seven out of ten people who set up business on their own fail within the year whereas nine out of ten franchises survive. Examine the reason for this. (AEB, June 1987)

2. Is it possible for business ethics to help firms achieve increased profits, or are such ethics expensive luxuries which few firms can afford in today's competitive environment? (AEB, Nov 1987)

Small firms

Figure 2.1

Why so many firms go bust

INSOLVENCIES in the UK rose by close on 10 per cent last year – the first uptick since 1984.

According to Dun & Bradstreet, a total of 18,163 businesses went bust, with London and the South-east the worst hit areas. Only the North-west showed a reduction compared with 1988.

My colleague Christopher Morris, who specialises in liquidations, warns it is unlikely that the upsurge in the current level of liquidations will decline during 1990.

High rates of interest, the impact of ever-increasing business rates and increases in the cost of salaries and services can be expected to cause numerous failures.

The message from Morris, however, is: 'The banks are now much more sophisticated in dealing with problem lending. An early approach to the bank for help or advice can make all the difference between survival and failure.'

If you ask someone whose business has become insolvent, gone into liquidation or just faded away: 'What happened? What went wrong?', he is likely to say: 'We ran out of money.' If pressed, he might well add: 'There really wasn't a market for our goods, our debtors wouldn't pay up, the competition was far too hot and the business was not very well situated. We were also undercapitalised and staff costs were just too high.'

In most cases, such responses are cover-ups for bad management. Business failure is usually a failure of people to plan or do something which might have prevented failure.

Owner-manager failures fall under four main headings:

Incompetence – no basic knowledge and skills to plan, manage and control the business;

Lack of management experience – not enough experience in supervising people and the jobs they do;

Unbalanced experience – considerable formal education, but little or no practical experience of the particular industry in which they have chosen to operate;

Personal weaknesses – the entrepreneur may not be cut out to run his own business. He may fail to make contacts; have difficulty communicating with people, organising and motivating employees and adjusting to the realities of a business that may be less attractive than anticipated.

Business difficulties are often reflected in alcoholism, breakdowns and marital problems. Running a venture can consume the energies, emotions and time of the entrepreneur; he has little to give elsewhere and therefore other commitments tend to suffer.

He may lose (or may never have had) the commitment and perseverance essential for running a successful and prosperous business.

The entrepreneur must be aware of the weaknesses which can cause a business to fail. He must acknowledge and understand the risks involved in running a business which if not properly managed may bring about his downfall.

● **No professional advice.** Cash is a limiting factor for many entrepreneurs, and they are often conspicuously slow to seek expert advice from accountants, marketing consultants and others because they consider it expensive and unnecessary.

Many seem to rely heavily on informal business contacts whose advice may lead to bad decisions. There is a natural reluctance to seek advice after mistakes have been made. The time for advice is before making mistakes.

● **Inadequate financial resources.** A business may fail if there are insufficient capital and loan facilities or a wrong mix of finance, for example, too much loan capital with interest charges which cannot be absorbed. Or the available resources may have been exhausted on property, expensive equipment and cars without making sufficient provision for day-to-day working capital.

An initially viable financial plan may become untenable if there is overtrading or a delay in building up the business.

● **Lack of financial management and discipline.** Financial control is dependent upon accurate information about cash flow, profits and costs.

If there is no regular financial monitoring, inefficient or improper use of the available resources may result.

● **Poor decision-making and planning.** Many owner-managers do not plan ahead. Problems are dealt with on a day-to-day basis and no decisions – or the wrong decisions – are made. They have not learned to delegate responsibility, nor has time and money been spent on training. Although not qualified, they attempt to do everything themselves.

● **Lack of technical skills.** A poor product or service – possibly produced at an uncompetitive price – can reflect inadequate or out-of-date technology or untrained staff.

● **Poor marketing research and strategy.** More business failures are attributed to sales and marketing than to administration.

Some so-called businesses never have a chance of success; they may be the founder's hobby, there may be no demand for the product or it may be impossible to produce it at a competitive price. The market may be notorious for bad debts or extended credit terms.

● **Expansion without planning.** Entrepreneurs have an inbuilt urge to expand, but often fail to appreciate that expansion requires careful planning. Symptoms include an inability to match the production of goods or services with sales, excessive demands on cash resources, a breakdown of accounting, over-extended management.

Expansion may highlight other latent weaknesses, for example, a failure to delegate or a failure to exercise financial control.

● **Wrong location.** Cheap premises in the wrong area may be a false economy, creating transport costs and staff shortage. On the other hand, many businesses have moved to larger, grander premises from a modest railway arch, only to fail.

Some of these causes of failure are more important than others. Under-capitalisation, managerial incompetence and personality defects are prime causes and cannot usually be compensated for by other assets or plus factors.

Adequate finance and managerial competence are essential but they must be supplemented by motivation, hard work, persistence and flexibility along with a good product or innovative idea.

Brian Jenks is the partner responsible for private companies at Touche Ross.

(Observer, 11 February 1990)

Figure 2.2

The very model of a modern minor enterprise

WHILE many small and medium-sized enterprises are currently experiencing difficulties, there are some which continue to thrive.

Recently it was my privilege to be part of one such success story. In 1986 a young man called Jeremy Hill was visiting California and noticed that the supermarket cold-cabinets had screens in front to stop the cold air escaping. The screens were made of transparent PVC strips which enabled customers to remove produce from the cabinets.

Jeremy was immediately convinced that this was a viable business idea. In 1986 the main saleable benefit from chiller strips was power conservancy. Hygiene and temperature control were not major issues.

So convinced was Jeremy that on his return to England he gave up his job and set up business with a colleague to market the product. They did not succeed, mainly because the business was short of capital and did not win enough customers who recognised the benefits of the product.

Jeremy remained undeterred and it was not long before he and his wife Sue formed a new company to market virtually the same product – after all, it was the trend in the US.

If you fail the first time try again.

It proved very hard work. Jeremy and Sue worked seven days a week to assemble the chiller strip blinds in their garage. Jeremy also visited customers to install the blinds and looked for new customers. They were convinced that they had found a niche market in which there was very little competition.

The product also had the advantage of topicality. In 1989 their efforts were assisted by the publicity in respect of food hygiene. Salmonella scandals, Edwina Currie's egg campaign and the fact that customers would no longer tolerate melting packs of butter on food shelves led to a demand for legislation. As a result, from 1 April next year most dairy products will have to be stored in conditions that ensure a product temperature of 8 degrees Celsius or less.

Two successive hot summers in 1989 and 1990 reinforced the case for dairy products to be kept in cool conditions which were attractive to the customer. There were significant electricity savings for shops and supermarkets which installed the chiller strips.

Jeremy decided to submit the chiller blinds for BS Standards Institution tests. While the outlay of £5,000 was significant the satisfactory result provided proof that chiller strips worked, that temperatures were kept to required levels and that there was a major power saving. The BSI's endorsement was recorded in Jeremy and Sue's brochures and sales literature.

Further tests, carried out by the Institute of Food Research on behalf of the Ministry of Agriculture, Fisheries and Food, confirmed that the blinds provided a relatively inexpensive method of temperature control.

In 1990 the business expanded. Jeremy and Sue adopted the approach that an order should not be turned away, providing they were satisfied that the customer was going to pay the bill. This sometimes meant sending the chiller blinds to the customer with installation instructions rather than fitting them themselves.

Jeremy and Sue slowly expanded their staff. They invited their sales manager, Ken Patel, to become a director and shareholder and gave him a national role. They took on extra sales staff and built up a team of assemblers and fitters. A staff bonus scheme was instituted with the result that they have a keen and happy work-force who are 100 per cent behind the business.

Sue, who was responsible for the heavy burden of book-keeping, invoicing and office administration, threatened to be overwhelmed. But although invoicing and debt collection fell behind, she remained in control and ensured that matters such as the VAT return were completed on time.

Last spring Jeremy and Sue realised that they could not continue to operate from a garage in the London suburbs and moved to a site in Cambridgeshire. It was easier to find good quality staff and pay rates were significantly lower than in the London area.

From time to time Jeremy had to act against 'poachers' and would-be competitors. In one instance someone had used an extract from his brochure claiming a 47 per cent power saving with chiller strips and in another Jeremy's photographs had been used. In both cases their solicitors acted quickly.

The new premises offer room for expansion. Jeremy believes he can produce as many as 1,000 blinds per week; with 500,000 food shops in the UK and half of those suitable candidates for chiller screens the potential market is large.

Jeremy has employed an in-house accountant and plans to export to Europe.

It is likely that the EC will follow the Government and introduce legislation which requires dairy products to be stored at a temperature similar or perhaps lower than those to be adopted in the UK.

Jeremy already has a new product in mind to enable the business to expand beyond simply chiller strips.

When Jeremy came to my office recently his first words were: 'It is very hard work, and I do not want to continue at this pace indefinitely.'

Turnover this year is likely to be some £1.5 million, so Jeremy, Sue and Ken Patel have an investment of real value.

With hindsight it seems that Jeremy and Sue made mistakes, but they have been right about many things.

Their business can be taken as a model for a start-up.

cont.

Figure 2.2 (continued)

Primarily Jeremy was the right man: he had commitment; knowledge of the product and the market. He believed that a market niche existed for his product. Chiller strips could be sold as a method of power saving, to meet food temperature control requirements and because they improved the appearance of food stored in cabinets. Certainly Edwina Currie and two hot summers played their part.

Jeremy saw that there was a large market for his product and very little competition. In such circumstances it was essential that the product and his service were high quality rather than price-sensitive.

Jeremy and Sue made it a priority to have well motivated staff. As well as a bonus scheme, employees have benefited from training courses organised by Leadership Development. It was also a priority to keep customers happy, so they never turned orders away.

Although credit control, invoicing, debt collection and the bank arrangements may have suffered, it has not been a major concern, because their priorities have been to look after the product, staff and customers.

They have not stood still with one product and one market. They have plans to expand into Europe and introduce a second product. They will be strengthening their management team and ensuring that they have adequate information on which to base decisions.

Finance has not been a problem so far because the business has a very positive cash flow. With their track record it should not be a problem to obtain bank facilities or investor participation, if needed, during the next stage of expansion.

I hope the story of Jeremy and Sue is an encouragement to those who have a business idea and see a market for it. While more businesses are going bust than a year ago the committed entrepreneur should persevere.

(*Observer*, 14 Sept. 1990)

SHORT-ANSWER QUESTIONS

1. If someone says that their business failed because 'we ran out of money' then what aspects of bad management could have accounted for this?
2. Why do you think that owner-managers whose businesses fail through incompetence are attracted to the idea of starting their own business in the first place?
3. Why might an aspiring owner-manager be advised not to rely too heavily upon a formal business education?
4. Why might those owner-managers who believe that professional advice is an unnecessary expense be the very people who are most in need of such advice?
5. What is the importance of achieving the correct mix between different types of finance?
6. Why will too much emphasis upon fixed assets at the expense of working capital create problems for a new firm?
7. Assume that a business' initial sales are much higher than anticipated. What factors should an owner-manager consider before an immediate expansion of the business?
8. To what extent would you agree with the view that some formal training in financial management is a priority skill for owner-managers?
9. Why might owner-managers hesitate to delegate responsibility and decision-making and how can this affect a business?
10. Why do you think so many new businesses fail by neglecting such an obvious factor as potential market demand and other aspects of marketing?

ANALYSING BUSINESS SITUATIONS

1. What are the strengths of a good supervisor? Describe the ways in which a lack of supervisory skills can affect the costs and reputation of a new business.
2. Give examples of those aspects of setting up and managing a business where the personal, social and communications skills of the owner are of particular importance.
3. Outline the factors which have given the Hills' product such a large potential market. Why is the demand for their product not likely to be affected by a general fall in the level of consumer spending?
4. Why was there a need for the Hills to tighten the firm's financial arrangements?
5. In the light of the various reasons 'Why so many firms go bust', identify with examples the different personal and management skills which have contributed to the success of the Hills' business.

ACTIVITIES

LOCAL STUDY

Each student should select a small manufacturing company in the local area which can be used as a basis for further investigation into small businesses. The small units based upon premises previously occupied by a large industrial concern or small firms sited on a business park are a good starting-point. Both of these are likely to have relatively new small companies.

In carrying out your investigation you should include the following steps:

(a) Obtain a copy of the firm's sales brochure to get to know its products and the kinds of manufacturing processes involved.
(b) Identify the firm's market.
(c) Arrange to meet the owner or one of the partners of the business to find out why and how the business was originally set up and how it has developed since then.
(d) To undertake (c) in a businesslike way you should prepare a series of questions based upon the kinds of issues raised in the two articles that relate to the success or otherwise of small companies.

ESSAYS

1. The founder and owner of a small private company is concerned that his firm's profitability is highly dependent on one, technologically advanced, product. Discuss the strategies he may adopt. (AEB, June 1988)
2. Why is delegation so necessary to the success of a business, and why is it so difficult to carry out? (AEB, June 1988)
3. (a) Explain the benefits to a self-employed sole trader of forming a private limited company to conduct his business.
   (b) Discuss factors which would limit the size of a firm within an industry. (University of Cambridge, June 1989)

Toyota—local production

Figure 3.2

OVERVIEW OF TOYOTA

PROGRESS OF LOCAL PRODUCTION

Towards corporate citizenship the world over

We at Toyota have long held the belief that the best way to provide customers with the goods they need when they need them is to produce the goods where customers need them. To remain true to this ideal, we continue to develop new overseas projects.

Last year, in North America, production of passenger cars started in the U.S. and Canada by Toyota Motor Manufacturing, U.S.A. Inc. (TMM) and Toyota Motor Manufacturing Canada Inc. (TMMC) respectively. And in April of this year, a decision was made to produce pick-up trucks at New United Motor Manufacturing, Inc. (NUMMI).

In Europe, joint production with Volkswagen of pickup trucks in West Germany began in January 1989. Also, Toyota announced that it chose a site in U.K. for its passenger car production in Europe.

Other projects are under way around the world. Vehicle production continues in Taiwan, as does a joint venture with General Motors in Australia and production in the Philippines. Also in progress is a technical cooperation program with China in Shenyang.

Figure 3.1

Figure 3.3

The flow of overseas Toyota vehicles

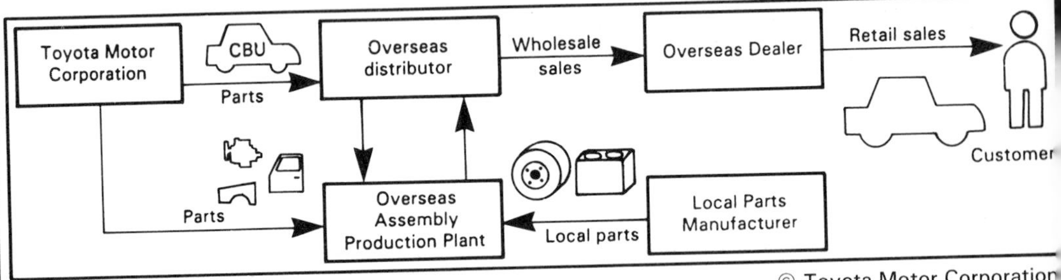

NOTE: CBU Complete Built-up Vehicles

Figure 3.4

Toyota aims at 6m production target despite industry warnings

By Kevin Done, Motor Industry Correspondent, in Derby

TOYOTA, the leading Japanese car maker, is planning to increase its worldwide vehicle production by almost a third to 6m units a year by the late 1990s, disclosed Mr Eiji Toyoda, group chairman, yesterday.

Toyota is stepping up its challenge to General Motors and Ford of the US for leadership of the world auto industry. This is despite recent warnings from leading western European car makers about an overcapacity of more than 8m units a year in the industry.

Mr Toyoda was speaking at the ground-breaking ceremony for Toyota's first European car plant – a £700m facility with a 200,000 unit annual capacity – to be built at Burnaston, near Derby.

He said the group was already close to achieving its initial target of a 10 per cent share of total world vehicle sales.

Toyota is the world's third-largest vehicle maker behind GM and Ford. Last year it produced 4.56m cars and commercial vehicles compared with factory sales of 6.34m by Ford and 7.9m by GM.

The US vehicle makers are coming under heavy pressure in their domestic market from Japanese producers.

Japanese car makers account for more than 25 per cent of US car sales, and their presence is also set to increase sharply in Europe this decade.

Mr Toyoda said that by the late 1990s Toyota was planning to increase its domestic Japanese car and truck production to about 4.5m from 3.98m in 1989.

The main thrust would be made overseas, however, where Toyota planned to increase production to about 1.5m a year from almost 600,000 in 1989 (including 117,000 vehicles assembled from kits supplied out of Japan).

Its planned sales by the late 1990s would be divided equally between the domestic and overseas markets with sales of 3m in each.

Other Japanese car makers are also aggressively expanding their overseas production bases. Car plants are under development in Europe by Toyota, Nissan and Honda.

John Griffiths adds: The Lexus LS400, Japan's first challenger in the UK luxury car market, goes on sale today at a price of £34,250, including tax.

Toyota, its manufacturer, regards the top models from Jaguar, BMW and Mercedes as the main rivals to the Lexus. It hopes to sell 600–700 cars this year and about 1,000 in 1991.

This is below targets set some months ago of 800–1,000 this year and 1,200 in 1991 – said to be the result of higher-than-expected sales in the US, where the Lexus made its debut in September.

(*Financial Times*, 5 June 1990)

Figure 3.5

Toyota breaks new ground towards 10,000 Welsh jobs

Martyn Halsall
Northern Industrial Correspondent

More than 10,000 jobs in Wales will be supported by Japanese companies when the £140 million Toyota engine plant opens on Deeside, North Wales, David Hunt, the Welsh secretary, said yesterday.

Wales is home for more than 20 Japanese companies and he will be seeking to bring more to the principality when he visits Japan later this year, he revealed during a 'ground breaking ceremony' which formally began work on the 115-acre Toyota site.

The plant will be Toyota's first European engine plant. Production of 1800cc engines for the new Toyota car plant at Burnaston, Derbyshire is due to start in mid-1992. The first Toyotas will roll off the production lines in Derbyshire later that year.

Two hundred people will work on Deeside during the plant's first phase, eventually increasing to 300. The plant will be on reclaimed marshland, the site of a former steelworks, and will initially produce about 100,000 engines a year.

Mr Hunt said: 'Wales has built something of a reputation for having good relationships with Japanese industry and I believe that it has one of the largest concentrations of Japanese industry in Europe.' Japanese companies were welcome in Wales, 'and there is always room for more', he said.

Mr Tatsuro Toyoda, executive vice-president of the Toyota Motor Corporation, said the engine plant would be a hi-tech facility 'with its quality-first automatic machining, assembly and inspection lines'.

He skirted earlier anxieties about 'local' (European) content and hostility in parts of the EC to vehicles produced by Japanese companies in Britain. He said Toyota in Britain was 'a truly British company, making a valuable contribution to the economies of the United Kingdom and Europe'.

Recruitment for the new engine plant will begin in mid-1991, in an area which lost 8,000 jobs in steel and associated closures 10 years ago.

(*Guardian*, 4 July 1990)

INVESTIGATION OF BUSINESS TERMS

Joint venture. A situation where two business organizations work together in an economic activity which may draw upon and combine their respective levels of technical and commercial expertise, research and development skills, investment funds and production facilities.

Technical co-operation programme. A situation where two business organizations combine their technical expertise and carry out joint research and development activities for a particular product.

Overseas distributor. An individual or business organization which holds and distributes stocks of a particular imported product. In many cases the distributor operates as a wholesaler for the overseas dealer who actually sells to the customer.

Overcapacity. A situation where a particular industry has the productive capability to produce more of a good or service than the market requires.

Unit annual capacity. The number of units of a particular product that a business organization in particular, or industry in general, is capable of producing in one year.

SHORT-ANSWER QUESTIONS

1. What is the objective in terms of customer satisfaction behind Toyota's expansion overseas?
2. Identify the two ways in which Toyota exports its vehicles into overseas markets.
3. Give three examples of how Toyota has expanded its operations abroad through integration.
4. Which particular sector of the UK car market has Toyota targeted for its main competitive thrust?
5. Give two reasons for the overcapacity that exists in the European car industry.
6. Why might overseas governments be more prepared to accept imports of Toyota kits rather than complete built-up vehicles?

ANALYSING BUSINESS SITUATIONS

1. Examine the business objectives behind the setting up of Toyota's first European car plant at Burnaston near Derby.
2. How is Toyota stepping up its challenge to General Motors and Ford of the United States for leadership of the world auto industry?
3. What are the locational advantages for Toyota of placing its engine plant on Deeside?
4. Why should David Hunt, the Welsh Secretary, be so keen to encourage Japanese companies to locate in Wales?
5. Examine the short and long-term advantages to Wales of Toyota locating its engine plant on Deeside.
6. Why should there be such hostility within Europe towards vehicles produced by Japanese companies in Britain?

ACTIVITIES

INVESTIGATION

(a) Obtain a copy of the Central Statistical Office's *Regional Trends*.
(b) Study the relevant regional profile and subregional statistics.
(c) Make out a case to justify:
   (i) Toyota's decision to locate its engine plant on Deeside.
   (ii) The Welsh Secretary's support for Toyota's decision to come to Deeside.

ESSAYS

1. Examine the particular problems posed for a country by the existence of multinational firms. (AEB, Nov. 1987)
2. Discuss the view that all business decisions taken by multinationals have an international rather than national perspective.
3. Examine the statement that the major objective of any multinational is to stay in business.
4. Explain how multinationals may reduce their business risks through diversification.

British Rail

Figure 4.1

Fares set to rise 12pc as BR profits slump

FARES are almost certain to rise by 12 per cent in the New Year even though British Rail showed a profit of almost £270 million, down from £304 million the previous year, in its annual report yesterday.

It would have lost £142 million, despite subsidies of almost £587 million, without property deals which raised a record £412 million in the year ended March 31.

InterCity and Railfreight, both operating without subsidies, were profitable but there were losses of £509 million on Provincial passenger trains, £138 million on Network SouthEast and almost £16 million on Parcels.

'Profit after asset sales was the third highest ever recorded and investment topped £700 million for the first time,' Sir Bob Reid, the chairman of BR, said.

The slowdown in the economy was making it harder for BR to meet financial targets set by Government, he said in a clear warning that fares will have to rise by more than the rate of inflation.

Last year's strikes cost £83 million, causing an operating loss on railways for the first time since the pit strike in 1984.

Sir Bob said BR had reduced its need for subsidies even faster than the Government had requested. Taxpayers provided just over £500 million and ratepayers put in another £91 million last year, compared with government rail subsidies of £4 billion in Italy, £3.5 billion in West Germany and £3 billion in France.

BR expects the Government to pay for extra safety measures required following the inquiry into the triple crash at Clapham. The price is still being assessed, but could be £800 million.

(*Daily Telegraph*, 5 July 1990)

Figure 4.2

Rail report condemns decline in BR support

THE GOVERNMENT is expected to come under attack this week for its policies towards British Rail. A report by the Central Transport Consultative Committee, the body which checks on BR's activities, is highly critical about the lack of long-term strategic planning for the service.

And it expresses concern about 'the continual remorseless decline in the support BR receives', according to Maj-Gen Lennox Napier, the committee chairman.

The committee's annual report is embargoed until tomorrow, but Maj-Gen Napier was responding to an article in *The Sunday Correspondent* which described the report as 'a devastating indictment of the way government cuts are hitting BR's services'.

He said the report acknowledged that BR had improved its performance 'despite not having all the tools to do the job'.

He added that long-term strategic decisions would have to be made soon about BR's 'mega-projects' if the travelling public was to have the sort of railway needed in the 1990s and beyond.

'The report is a firm encouragement to the Government to come clean on the long-term strategic future of BR and to make firm clear decisions so we the passengers and BR really know where we are going over the next 10 years,' Maj-Gen Napier said.

The report also warns against any further decline in the so-called public service obligation grant, saying that if it declines further the quality and quantity of services are bound to suffer.

'We are concerned about the continual remorseless decline in the support that British Rail receives,' he said.

(*Independent*, 30 July 1990)

Figure 4.3

The culture of British Rail

THE simple if daunting task for Sir Bob Reid and Mr John Welsby, the new chairman and chief executive of British Rail, is to change the culture and improve the efficiency of the railways. This task will entail increases in the quality and quantity of BR's management, so that it can handle the growing investment programme required by rising traffic and a more affluent travelling public, and a transformation in the pay structure for the rest of its staff. The aim must be to escape from the present combination of low hourly pay and long hours of work and to create a highly productive and well-paid labour force.

Working practices

BR began large-scale recruitment of managers from outside under Sir Robert Reid, its previous chairman; continuing to recruit managers and engineers remains the first priority for BR, although it may be able to alleviate the problem by sub-contracting more work to suppliers. But it also needs to transform working practices among its staff. Its staff should be employed for the hours they are required – which in the nature of a railway service are liable to be morning, evening and weekend rather than nine to five – and then paid a competitive hourly rate.

Realities recognised

BR is now seeking to achieve contracts of employment which recognise these realities for about half its staff. The unions have accepted the principle, but are bargaining hard over the payment their members will require for these changes. They should recognise that BR cannot be transformed into a high-productivity, high-pay employer unless it can pay staff only for the time that they are doing useful work. If it can do so, and can vary pay locally to reflect demand, it should be able to obtain the quantity and quality of staff it requires. The reforms are as much in the interest of the unions' members as in the interest of the taxpayer.

(*Financial Times*, 1 Aug 1990)

Subsidies. Payments made by the government which form a wedge between the price consumers pay and the costs incurred by the producer of a good or service. The subsidy has the effect of keeping the price below the marginal cost. In the case of the nationalized industries the subsidy was traditionally used to keep the price at a level which the majority of people could reasonably be expected to afford.

Public Service Obligation Grant. Grants paid by central government to compensate British Rail for losses incurred in the operation of uncommercial passenger services at the request of government. Such requests may have been made for strategic, commercial, social or environmental reasons.

Subcontracting. In order to fulfil the conditions of a contract between two parties, one of the parties may enter into further (or sub-) contracts with other parties in order to secure help in completing part or all of its side of the original contract.

Productivity. The level of output per unit of input employed. Productivity may be increased by improving the efficiency of either capital or labour.

SHORT-ANSWER QUESTIONS

1. Explain why British Rail was able to make a profit of almost £270 million during the financial year 1989/90.
2. Outline the fundamental differences in the way in which a public corporation such as British Rail conducts its financial affairs from the approach taken by a public limited company.
3. Describe the ways in which British Rail will have to alter the working practices of its staff in order to improve efficiency and productivity.
4. Why must the British Rail unions take a more flexible attitude towards wage bargaining if British Rail is to prosper as a business organization?
5. If British Rail were to be privatized which parts of its service would be most likely to come under threat and why?

ANALYSING BUSINESS SITUATIONS

1. What are the strategic, social, commercial and environmental arguments for the government continuing to support British Rail's operations?
2. Why might further reductions in the Public Service Obligation Grant reduce the actual quantity of rail services provided?
3. How might British Rail's operations be developed in the long-term as part of a totally integrated transport policy?
4. How could the government prevent the privatization of British Rail from resulting in considerable cuts in its services?

ACTIVITIES

LOCAL STUDY

Design a suitable questionnaire and conduct a survey to discover the views of the local community on the following aspects of British Rail's activities:

(a) The standard of train service from the local station in terms of frequency, reliability, destinations, car parking, advice and information, refreshments, cleanliness and safety.
(b) The extent to which any co-ordination exists between local train services and other forms of transport such as buses.
(c) Whether the train services might be expected to improve if they were moved into the private sector.

The class should combine its findings and use them as a basis for considering whether British Rail should ultimately be privatized.

ESSAYS

1. Examine the case for privatizing British Rail and suggest how it might be brought about.
2. 'Privatization through the profit motive ultimately maximizes consumer satisfaction.'

'Certain industries are too important to be left in private ownership.'

From your study of business, how far can you reconcile these two views? (AEB, Nov. 1988)

3. 'Since its nationalization British Rail has never been allowed by successive governments to fulfil its true objectives.' Discuss this statement.

Virgin

Figure 5.1

VIRGIN GROUP OF COMPANIES – CORPORATE HISTORY

1968 26 January, first issue of *Student Magazine*, Richard Branson's first business venture.

1970 Start of Virgin mail-order operation.

1971 First Virgin record shop opens in Oxford Street.

1972 First Virgin recording studio opens at 'The Manor' near Oxford, England.

1973 Virgin Record Label launched, with first signing Mike Oldfield whose album 'Tubular Bells' became one of the biggest selling of the decade. The album was used as the soundtrack to the international hit movie – 'The Exorcist'.

1977 Virgin signs the Sex Pistols after both EMI and A & M have decided they are too hot to handle.

1978 First Virgin nightclub opens, The Venue, Clubs later became part of the Voyager Group.
Human League signed to Virgin.

1980 Virgin Records expanding presence in overseas markets; initially on a licensing basis and leads to the establishment of own subsidiaries, firstly in France and, later on, in all major territories.

1981 Phil Collins signed to Virgin label for UK.

1982 Boy George (Culture Club) signed to Virgin for worldwide rights.

1983 Virgin Vision (forerunner of the communications business) formed to distribute films and videos and operate in television and broadcasting sector.

1984 Virgin Atlantic Airways launched. Virgin now flies to New York (Newark and Kennedy), Miami, Orlando, Los Angeles, Boston, Moscow and Tokyo.

1985 £25 million private placing of 7 per cent convertible stock completed with 25 English and Scottish institutions (September).
Virgin wins Business Enterprise Award for company of the year. Companies now include record labels, retail outlets, exporting music publishing, broadcasting, satellite television, video and film distribution.
Following an acquisition in October, Vision distributes film and video in Europe, USA, Australia and Far East.

1986 Virgin Group, comprising the Music, Retail and Property and Communications divisions, floated (November) on London Stock Exchange, with 35 per cent of the ordinary equity being acquired by 87,000 shareholders. Airline, clubs, holidays and aviation services remain part of privately-owned company called Voyager Group Limited. Virgin Group operating in 17 countries employing over 1600 people.

1987 Virgin Records America launched. Investment in new US record labels key to development of worldwide music coverage, quickly followed by establishment of subsidiary in Japan.
Virgin Vision Inc launched, following the reorganisation of film and video distribution activities in the US.
BSB (British Satellite Broadcasting), of which Virgin Group, Granada, Anglia and Pearson were founder members, was awarded UK licence for direct broadcast by satellite in the UK to broadcast five new TV channels commencing autumn 1989.
Acquisition of W.H. Allen, publishing company. A 45 per cent stake acquired in Mastertronics Group. Virgin Mastertronics later became a wholly owned subsidiary primarily marketing and distributing computer games, software and consoles in several European countries.
First annual results as public company are above expectations at £28 million pre-tax on continuing businesses, on a turnover of £279 million.
Virgin obtains listing in USA on the NASDAQ Exchange and establishes a Euro-dollar and Sterling Commercial Paper programme.

1988 Biography of Richard Branson published, author Mick Brown.
Virgin Atlantic announces profits for 1987 of £5 million.
Olympic recording studios opened in Barnes, London. Most modern studio complex in Europe.
New international record label – Virgin Classics – established to specialise in high quality classical repertoire.
Opening of first Virgin Megastore in Australia, largest 'Entertainment Superstore' in the continent.
Smaller UK retail outlets sold to W.H. Smith Group for £23 million. Concentration of retail strategy on Megastores with new openings in Glasgow (Dec. 1988) and Paris (Nov. 1988) to be followed by megastores in numerous other British, European and Pacific Basin cities.
Virgin Broadcasting formed as a subsidiary of Virgin Communications Ltd to further develop Virgin's interests in radio and television.
Virgin Atlantic Airways wins three major business class awards for its Upper Class across the Atlantic and the airline becomes Britain's primary long-haul operator after British Airways.
Richard Branson announces Management Buyout following the October 1987 stock market crash. Offer of 140p per share in October 1988 valuing the Group at £248 million was accepted by the 41,000 shareholders and Virgin Group joined Voyager Group as a private company in January 1989.
Superchannel acquired by Videomusic of Italy. Virgin retains 42 per cent of the equity, the channel now accesses over 20 million homes throughout Europe.
Virgin sells its shareholding in BSB to Bond Corporation at a profit.

1989 Virgin Atlantic announces doubled pre-tax profits at £10 million.
Virgin Mastertronics signs long term European Distribution for Sega Video Games (later becomes European leader).
Voyager Travel Holdings, holding company for Virgin Atlantic Airways, sells 10 per cent of its equity to Seibu Saison International, one of Japan's largest retail and travel groups, in return for an injection of £36 million of equity and convertible loan capital.
Virgin Vision sold to Management Company Entertainment Group (MCEG) of Los Angeles for $83 million, $55 million of which was received in cash.
Virgin Music Group enters investment partnership with Fujisankei Communications Group. The $5 billion Japanese media group pays £100 million for a 25 per cent stake. New record companies in the Far East and the USA planned.
Virgin Atlantic Airways establishes its own engineering operations.
Virgin Retail France sells a 38 per cent equity holding to Paribas, Credit Agricole and Saulnes-Chatillon.

1990 Virgin Music Group launches New York based record company following success of Virgin Records America launched in Los Angeles 1987.
Virgin Retail Group and Marui Company of Japan announce the formation of a new 50:50 joint venture company to operate a chain of megastores in Japan. The first outlet opened in Shijuku, Tokyo on 22 September.
Other new magastores open in Marseilles (May), Bordeaux (October) and Belfast (October).
Virgin Retail Europe sells a 20 per cent equity holding to ASKO, Paribas and Canal +.

1991 Richard Branson and Per Lindstrand successfully cross the Pacific in the world's largest hot air balloon, breaking all existing ballooning distance and speed records.
Virgin Atlantic wins historic ruling by the CAA allowing it to operate extra services to Tokyo. Virgin Atlantic wins the right to operate services out of Heathrow (London) in addition to Gatwick (London). The airline also wins new route licences to Orlando, Washington, Chicago and San Francisco.
Virgin Atlantic Airways commences new service to Boston.

By kind permission of Will Whitehorn, Virgin Group of Companies

Figure 5.2

THE VIRGIN GROUP OF COMPANIES

Virgin consists of 4 separate holding companies involved in distinct business areas from music, media and publishing to retail, travel and leisure
There are over 120 operating companies across the 4 holding companies in 23 countries worldwide

Virgin Music Group *1	Virgin Retail Group	Virgin Communications	Virgin Holdings: Virgin Group	Virgin Holdings: Voyager Group
Record companies in 20 countries, labels include Virgin, Virgin Classics, 10, Siren, Circa and Charisma Music Publishing Recording Studios	Operates a chain of megastores in the UK, Europe, Australia and Far East selling music, video and other entertainment products Wholesale record exports and imports	Distribution of Computer Games and Consoles Investments in Video and Film Distribution TV Post production services 525 Investments in book and Magazine publishing	Investments in broadcasting activities and joint-ventures (SuperChannel, Music Box) Rapido TV, Oui FM Property Development Management & Corporate Finance Services to the Virgin Organisation	Clubs & Hotels Airship & Balloon Operations Storm Model Agency Voyager Travel Holdings *2 UK's second largest long international airline (Virgin Atlantic Airways) Freight Handling and Packaging Inclusive tour operations (Virgin Holidays)

MAIN OPERATING COMPANIES OF EACH HOLDING COMPANY

Virgin Records Virgin Music Publishing Virgin Studios Associated Virgin Labels (AVL) Virgin Classics	Virgin Retail Virgin Retail Europe (80%) Virgin Retail France (62%) Caroline International Virgin Retail Far East	Virgin Mastertronic West One Television Rushes W.H. Allen & Co PLC 525 The Design Clinic	Vanson Developments Virgin Management Virgin Broadcasting Kiss-FM (28.05%) Oui FM (17.27%)	Virgin Atlantic Airways Virgin Holidays Virgin Aviation Services Voyager Hotels Airship & Balloon Company Storm Model Agency (50%)

Note: Marui Company of Japan own 50% of Virgin Megastores Japan Ltd.

Note *1: Fujisankei Communications Group of Japan has a 25 per cent equity investment in Virgin Music Group which is the sixth largest record company and largest independent in the World

Note *2: Seibu Saison International of Japan has a 10 per cent equity investment in Voyager Travel Holdings

Figure 5.3

VIRGIN GROUP OF COMPANIES TODAY

The Group currently employs over 6000 staff, operates directly in over 20 countries in the international media, entertainment, communications and travel businesses.

There are four independent parent companies: Music, Communications, Retail, and Holdings.

VIRGIN MUSIC GROUP

Virgin Music Group is the holding company within Virgin responsible for activities in music. It is currently the sixth largest record company and the largest independent music group in the world.

Virgin Record Companies operate in over 20 countries worldwide obtaining rights from artistes to exploit, in return for a royalty, the copyright in their recordings.

Virgin's Music Publishing companies contract with songwriters for the use of copyright material. The companies' aim is to ensure that compositions are recorded and further used in other media such as film and video and recording of the same song by different artistes.

Virgin Studios operates recording studio complexes in London and Oxford plus one mobile unit.

VIRGIN COMMUNICATIONS

Electronic Publishing and Distribution
Virgin Mastertronic is a publisher of computer, video and multimedia software in Europe and the US, and distributor for Sega video games which is the European market leader. It has offices in the UK, US, France, Germany and Spain.

Television provides post-production services to the advertising, broadcasting and video industries through several subsidiaries including West One Television, Rushes (TV post-production company acquired in 1987). Indiedit and 525 in Los Angeles.

Book Publishing
Virgin Books which has now been merged with wholly owned W.H. Allen and is a publisher of non-fiction hardback and paperback books.

Investments
VCL has interests in a small number of related activities including MCEG Virgin Vision Limited (film and video distribution), John Brown Publishing Limited (publisher of Viz – the UK's fastest growing magazine with a circulation of over one million), Limelight Film and Video (a leading producer of feature films, commercials and pop promos), Visage (a corporate communications company) and FM Design.

VIRGIN RETAIL GROUP

This holding company is responsible for the operation of a retail chain consisting to date, of 12 megastores in the major cities of the UK and 8 international outlets. International stores have been opened in Ireland, Australia, France and Japan, and are planned for other countries around the world with a particular emphasis on Europe and the Pacific Basin.

In the UK, Virgin has also launched a unique chain of Virgin Games stores which sell board games, hobby games and computer games hardware and software. So far 4 outlets have opened and up to 30 are planned.

Caroline Exports is a major independent importer and exporter of music and related products around the world.

The group has a number of partners in its overseas subsidiaries as follows: 20 per cent of Virgin Retail Europe is owned by ASKO, Paribas and Canal +; 38 per cent of Virgin Retail France is owned by Paribas, Credit Agricole and Saulnes-Chatillon; and 50 per cent of Virgin Megastores Japan is owned by Marui.

VIRGIN HOLDINGS

Broadcasting encompasses the group's investments in both radio and television programming including 42 per cent investment in Super Channel (Pan-European Broadcasting Service), Music Box, and other interests and joint ventures including programme production. Most recently, Kiss-FM, a new radio station has awarded a franchise for broadcasting in London. Virgin owns 20 per cent of the equity of this new venture.

Property Development
Vanson Developments Ltd began as a natural adjunct to Virgin's retailing business and as expertise in this area has grown a wide range of projects has been undertaken in the residential and commercial sectors.

Voyager Travel

Virgin Atlantic Airways is the main operating subsidiary of Voyager Travel Holdings, an intermediary holding company for a number of travel and leisure businesses including Virgin Holidays and Virgin Cargo.

The aim of the airline has always been to offer passengers a real choice by creating a unique value added quality product consisting of only two classes. Upper and Economy class, which respectively offer a high standard of service at a lower price than competitors.

Voyager Clubs and Hotels

Operates a number of clubs, venues and hotels.

Financial Information

The figures below indicate the total sales (turnover) for the four holding companies which make up the Virgin organisation worldwide.

(Year end 31 July)		Revenue (Turnover) (£ million)	Sales (Turnover) US $ million*
1984		94	160
1985		138	235
1986		240	408
1987		339	576
1988		475	808
1989		625	1022
1990		780	1224
1991	(projected)	1,100	1737

* Converted at 1.70 average rate

This growth in sales has largely been achieved through organic growth with no major acquisitions. Virgin is now the second largest private group of companies in the UK.

By kind permission of Will Whitehorn, Virgin Group of Companies, 1990

INVESTIGATION OF BUSINESS TERMS

Management buy-out. When a company is faced with a takeover bid, or is in business difficulties, then its senior management may seek to acquire financial and thus operational control of the company by buying up its shares.

1987 October crash. This was a combination of international, political and economic developments which caused a large and dramatic fall in the general level of prices on stock exchanges throughout the world. During a period of 48 hours average prices fell by over 25 per cent.

Independent music group. Is one which is not connected with the giants, such as CBS, EMI or Columbia, which between them tend to dominate the music industry.

Royalty. A payment made by a company to the owner of a copyright covering printed material, a musical score or a computer program. Royalties may also be paid for the use of a patent on a product developed by another company.

INVESTIGATION OF BUSINESS TERMS

Holding company. One which has financial control over other companies which are known as its subsidiaries. Financial control is achieved by the holding of 51 per cent of the ordinary shares of the subsidiary, although often a holding of less than 50 per cent may give effective control. Each subsidiary has its own name and operates as a separate entity. However, due to the majority share holding of the holding company it may direct the policy of the subsidiary to fulfil its overall strategy.

Operating company. One which actually is involved in the business of making goods or supplying services as distinct from a holding company which is purely a financial concern with a controlling interest in others.

Equity investment. Refers to the holding of ordinary shares in a company and other classes of shares which are the most risky in that the return depends entirely upon the fortunes of the company.

Copyright. Refers to the sole right to reproduce printed material such as a book, an article or a musical composition. In effect it is monopoly control over the use of material.

Subsidiaries. Companies which are controlled by a holding company through its ownership of a sufficient number of ordinary shares.

Value-added product. Adding value to a basic service or product is achieved by improving the quality, standard, level and scope of a service, or in the case of a product furthering its level of processing or manufacturing. A service or product will therefore represent particularly good value for money if each time value is added there is not a corresponding increase in price.

Organic growth. Refers to expansion generated internally through a company's own resources and efforts, rather than development through the acquisition of existing businesses in the desired field.

SHORT-ANSWER QUESTIONS

1. Given the make-up of the Voyager Group why was it excluded from the flotation in 1986?
2. What factors might have led Richard Branson to repurchase the Virgin Group in January 1989?
3. Explain why Virgin has become increasingly involved in Japan and Japanese companies.
4. Why did Virgin decide to concentrate on the Megastore concept and sell its small retail outlets to W.H. Smith's in 1988?
5. Suggest why Virgin has on a number of occasions opted to expand by joint ventures.
6. What factors may have helped Virgin Atlantic Airways to operate so profitably when compared with the larger airlines?
7. Why has the Virgin Organization used a series of holding companies to control its diverse operations?
8. What factors may have helped the Virgin Music Group to survive as an independent in a market dominated by a few giant international companies?
9. Give some possible reasons why the Virgin Organization expanded through organic growth rather than through acquisitions.

ANALYSING BUSINESS SITUATIONS

1. Give some examples of the following kinds of integration:
   (a) forward vertical integration;
   (b) backward vertical integration;
   (c) horizontal organic growth;
   (d) lateral integration;
   (e) international expansion.

   In each case suggest the business advantages that arise out of these specific examples.
2. Explain how developments in technology have contributed to the growth and diversification of Virgin.
3. Calculate the percentage rate of growth in turnover for each of the years given. Give some possible reasons for the way in which it has changed.
4. Select one of the groups within the Virgin Organization and explain the business strategy behind its make-up.

ACTIVITIES

ROLE PLAY

(a) The class should be divided into five groups and each should be allocated one of the Virgin holding companies.

(b) The members of each holding company should then discuss:
- (i) those existing activities where there is a strong case for expansion;
- (ii) the scope that exists for diversifying into additional new lines of business;
- (iii) the benefits which (i) and (ii) would bring for other parts of the Virgin Organization.

(c) All holding companies should then attend a meeting at which each of them outlines and justifies their plans for expanding their existing operations or diversifying into new areas of business. The representatives of other holding companies should be prepared to question the reasoning and effects associated with such plans.

ESSAYS

1. Analyse the strategies available to a firm to enable it to survive a period of recession in its home market. (AEB, Nov. 1987)
2. Before 1981 management buy-outs were unknown in the UK. In 1986 there were 281 with a total value of £1.2 billion. Analyse the reasons for this growth. (AEB, June 1989)
3. Explain how recent technological developments have affected firms involved in supplying home entertainment products and related leisure activities.

Training for the future

Figure 6.1

Can TECs turn rags to riches?

Vince Harris is employee relations manager at GEC plc head office.
He is speaking at the Harrogate seminar on the future role of Training and Enterprise Councils.

As every personnel and training specialist knows, training in Britain is generally speaking a Cinderella business – at the stroke of midnight as the party ends and profits start to fall, the training department tends to be the first to discard its finery (if it ever had any) and flee for shelter. Remarkably, Training and Enterprise Councils may be uniting the decision-making princes of industry with the training Cinderellas, and this could be a fruitful if difficult match. In this article I want first to compare training in Britain to the achievements of our continental competitors and then to suggest some ideas which TECs may adopt to help Britain become more competitive.

Some may argue that, since we are already more competitive following the recession of the early to mid 1980s and the consequent shakeout, we need to train fewer people. Productivity has risen after all! But we already face serious skill shortages and, when we cross the Channel to consider what our competitors are doing, we realise the real seriousness of the situation and its consequences.

Within manufacturing industry, the numbers employed in France and Britain in electrical and electronic maintenance, installation and repair and mechanical engineering are roughly the same. For instance, France has 706,000 skilled employees in mechanical engineering compared to 765,000 in Britain. However, the percentage and numbers qualified are far higher in France than here. To take the above example, 55 per cent of France's skilled mechanical engineers have qualifications compared to 33 per cent in Britain. If we look at electrical and electronic maintenance we see that 40 per cent of the French workforce is employed at technician level – a level which does not exist in this country, due to demarcation and inflexibility in job specification.

But even among skilled workers only 43 per cent in Britain have a BTEC/ONC qualification or equivalent, or higher, compared with 74 per cent with this level of qualification in France.

Germany trained 78,000 people to craft level in mechanical and electrical engineering in 1975 and 25,000 to technician level. By 1987, these figures had risen to 89,000 and 45,000 respectively – roughly four times the numbers trained in the UK. Indeed, one company alone trains half as many apprentices every year as the entire British engineering industry.[2]

The position in engineering is not untypical in British industry. To enter retailing in Germany, to quote just one service sector example, some 40,000 school-leavers take a two-year apprenticeship leading to the equivalent of a craft qualification and a further 36,000 take a three-year course. The training will include commercial practice, double-entry book-keeping and law, in addition to the sort of product information that customers need. The effectiveness and thoroughness of the German training is evident to anyone entering a shop and may be one contributory factor to the high consciousness of quality among German consumers, whereas many in Britain all too often seek a low-priced, poor-quality 'bargain'.

Productivity between countries is difficult to compare, but the CBI in its economic review claimed that manufacturing productivity in France and Germany was ahead of Britain by 27 and 22 per cent respectively, while the corresponding figures for service industries were 22 per cent and 29 per cent respectively. There is persuasive evidence that these figures understate the situation. However, it is the wider consequences I now want to turn to.

In various comparative studies, Steedman, Prais and others from the National Institute for Economic and Social Research have revealed the direct causal connections between lower skill, lower productivity, and levels of training of employees in UK companies compared with their continental competitors. Some examples are:

1 Inadequate training means machine breakdowns in Britain take longer to fix and are a major cause of lost productivity. It is more common in Britain to resort to the supplier (usually an importer) to fix breakdowns which in France/Germany will often be repaired by supervisors or their subordinates.

2 Decision-making in Britain on proposals with a substantial technical content will frequently be made by those not technically qualified, who may even be suspicious of proposals they do not understand. Technological innovation thus becomes more difficult. In smaller companies major decisions may even be made by supervisors who are inadequately trained or even completely unqualified.

3 Product complexity in French/German businesses is often beyond the skill levels of their British counterparts. The simpler, lower added value products made by British companies will often be imported by their continental competitors from cheaper producers in the Far East. The clothing industry is a classic example where higher added value achieved by qualified operators results in an expanding German industry despite high pay levels, while the British industry competes with cheap labour in developing countries at a lower technological level, and is therefore still contracting.

4 It is more difficult to retrain a British workforce in new skills as our existing education system and the resulting skill base of people is often too narrow. This inevitably makes the realisation of people's full potential and capabilities more difficult and risky.

5 There is a greater division of responsibilities in Britain. Production, maintenance, production control and quality control will usually be under parallel management, leading to time delays when problems arise, and greater administrative complexity and higher costs.

6 There is a tendency to have more levels of management in Britain, possibly partly as a result of the above factors.

Inevitably, better-quality training depends on an adequate basic education. The former schools minister, John Butcher, said earlier this year that evidence from a recent survey showed that the average German 15-year-old was two years ahead of his or her British counterpart. In France 50 per cent of pupils leave school with the equivalent of GCSE Grade C in mathematics and French, plus seven other subjects. The current definition of GCSE grade E is the level the average 16-year-old in Britain will achieve – our school-leavers are two grades behind their French equivalents.

So what can the TECs do to improve British standards of education and training?

The TECs will above all be local bodies, led by people with an industrial and commercial expertise who are influential in the community they serve. The councils and their chief executives must be closely identified with the communities they serve, knowledgeable about the structure of local industry and its people problems, and they will need to establish close links with education providers at all levels. Some questions for TECs to ask will be: what are the existing skill shortages? Where will employment growth take place? What will be the impact of technology? What new industries should the locality try to attract or grow? What help can be given to schools? What are the strengths and weaknesses of other education providers in further and higher education? Can the local universities and polytechnics be encouraged to serve local industry better?

With skill shortages, the aim should not be to identify exact numbers to produce a manpower plan. A more strategic approach will be necessary, and this implies

gure 6.1 (continued)

oad-based training and plenty of

To ensure a properly skilled orkforce we must aim for a uantum leap in the numbers ualifying to NCVQ levels 3 and 4 craft and technician levels in engineering). An increase of 20 per cent, 30 per cent or even 50 per cent will be entirely inadequate. We should be aiming to get 50 per cent of school-leavers to this level, as opposed to less than 30 per cent at present.

Many TECs will also get involved in expanding the range of training facilities available to those returning to the labour market, particularly married women returners. They may want to promote the provision of crèche facilities and assist employers in developing accelerated training programmes for adults which recognise skills gained through experience. Operation of a training brokerage service, putting those with a training need in contact with providers for a fee, will be valued by many, particularly smaller, employers. TECs will also stimulate training networks of various kinds which will provide a pooling of employer-based expertise, and a sharing of facilities.

The CBI is promoting the idea of training vouchers, which would fit neatly into the jigsaw. Under this scheme, the individual would be entitled to a certain amount of training, purchased with the voucher. I suggest the training programme should need the agreement of the local employer or TEC, which would be concerned to ensure it was appropriate to the needs of local businesses.

Many people in the workforce, and even more outside it, will have left school under-educated with little by way of qualifications to show for their years at school. They cannot be left to become a forgotten generation – their talents must be developed and put to use. The TECs must be involved in imaginative ways, possibly using distance learning, including television, to improve their basic education, particularly in mathematics and science.

Finally, we must recognise that TECs are local and they can only address problems affecting the local labour market. When it comes to deficiencies in the national, let alone the European and international labour markets, a different solution is required. The engineering industry is especially concerned about a wide range of IT skills shortages, including some which are shared with other sectors of the economy. The national labour markets principally involve professional level skills (which typically require a degree level education), and there are problems here which are beyond the range of TECs as presently conceived. The UK cannot ignore them; they are too central to our ability to innovate, to develop new products and compete effectively in global markets.

But this should not detract from the significance of TECs, and every human resource manager must press his or her director to get involved – to help put Britain at least on a par with Europe, even though we will still be a long way behind Japan!

(Adapted from *Personnel Management* Oct. 1989)

References

1 *Employment for the 1990s*. Cm 540, HMSO, 1988.

2 All figures come from the series of five reports by the National Institute of Economic and Social Research (NIESR) published over the last six years. NIESR, 2 Dean Trench Street, Smith Square, London SW1P 3HE.

Figure 6.2 **PERCENTAGE OF MANUFACTURING FIRMS EXPECTING SHORTAGE OF SKILLED LABOUR TO LIMIT OUTPUT (January 1972 – July 1989).**

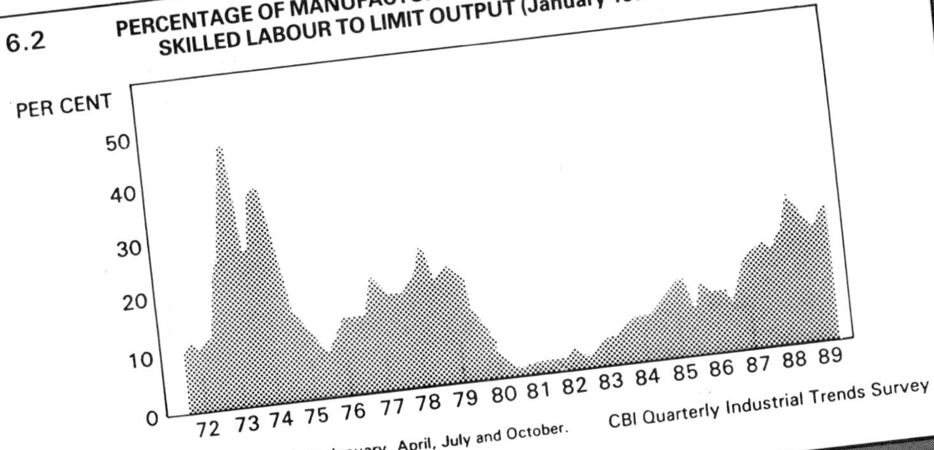

Note: The CBI Survey is carried out quarterly in January, April, July and October.

(Labour Market and Skill Trends, 1990/91)

Figure 6.3 **PERCENTAGE OF MANUFACTURING FIRMS REPORTING SKILL SHORTAGES AS LIMITING OUTPUT BY INDUSTRY**

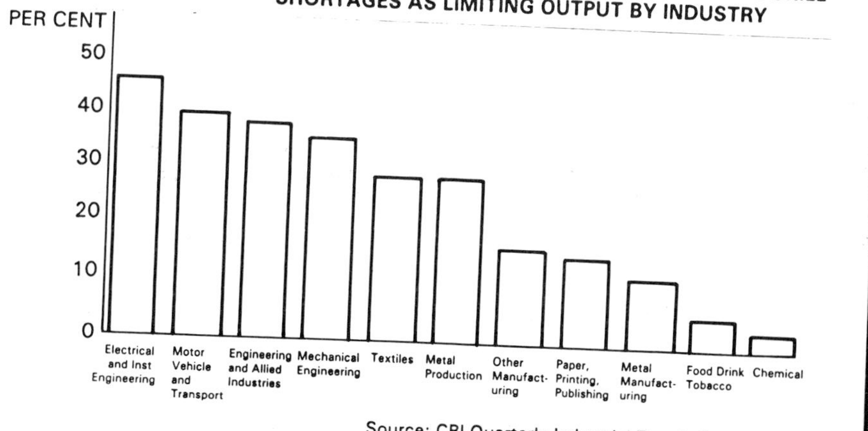

Source: CBI Quarterly Industrial Trends Survey: July 1989

(Labour Market and Skill Trends, 1990/91)

TECs (Training and Enterprise Councils). These first came into operation in 1990. A TEC consists of 12–15 members, two-thirds of whom should be drawn from the private sector. Its role is to analyse local training needs and skills shortages and then to identify appropriate training schemes in both the public and private sectors. At the time of their launch they were to have budgets of between £15m and £50m and 82 such TECs were to be established

Shake-out. This describes the shedding of labour during a recession when firms must pay particular attention to their labour costs. In these circumstances savings can be made through redundancies.

Demarcation. This is where the trade unions and groups of workers seek to clearly define types of jobs or tasks undertaken by their members.

Job specification. A detailed statement of what an employee does, what knowledge is used in doing this, the judgements made and the factors taken into account when making them.

Parallel management. A number of lines of management each reflecting a specialist area within a particular department. Any change within the department may involve the agreement of managers acting in parallel.

Manpower plan. This is a forecast of how many employees and kinds of skills will be required in the future, and to what extent this demand is likely to be met. This has implications for promotion and recruitment.

NCVQ. The National Council for Vocational Qualifications is a national body which accredits the certificates and diplomas awarded by such organizations as the City and Guilds of London Institute and the Royal Society of Arts. Its task is to develop a national structure for such qualifications and thus to improve the standards of vocational training in the UK, whether in schools and colleges or in the workplace.

SHORT-ANSWER QUESTIONS

1. Suggest why company spending on training tends to be the most prone to cuts when profits fall.
2. To what extent could it be argued that higher productivity helps to ease skills shortages?.
3. What would be the advantages to British industry of training more people to handle a greater range of decisions concerning different aspects of production management?
4. What training benefits might arise from the government attracting local business executives onto the boards of TECs?
5. Why might TECs be inappropriate for easing professional skills shortages?
6. At their launch in 1990, training credits were worth £1,500 and a school-leaver could buy this amount of training. Why might this encourage firms to do more training?

ANALYSING BUSINESS SITUATIONS

1. Give the reasons why a recession may contribute to improved productivity and hence greater competitiveness.
2. What is the advantage to French and German industry of having two levels of skills and qualifications? What is the cost to British industry of not having such a system?
3. Explain the suggested link between the level of training in Germany, the attitude of consumers and the quality of German products and services.
4. Why will training to deal with machine maintenance and breakdowns raise productivity?
5. Examine the case for more people at management and supervisory level in the UK having science or engineering backgrounds.
6. Argue the case for a greater emphasis on vocational education centred around a skills base that includes the following:

(a) numeracy
(b) literacy
(c) information gathering, analysis and presentation
(d) information technology
(e) working with others
(f) social and personal skills
(g) tackling problems.

7. 'The income received by TECs from the government will depend upon the number of NCVQ qualifications earned by trainees. Since all qualifications from NCVQ level 1 to level 4 will earn the same grant TECs may tend to concentrate upon these lower levels of training'. Discuss this statement in the light of the skill shortages highlighted in the article.
8. TEC boards must be comprised of chief executives and operational directors who are expected to devote one or two days a month of their time unpaid. Why, therefore, might the largest firms in the UK with centralized power structures find it difficult to get involved with TECs?

ACTIVITIES

INVESTIGATIVE ANALYSIS

1. By reference to such HMSO publications as the *Annual Abstract of Statistics* and the *National Income and Expenditure* blue book, identify the data which relate to changes in the output of various sections of the economy.

Use this information to explain the sudden rise/fall in the percentage of firms with skills shortages as in Figure 6.2.

2. By reference to such HMSO publications as the *Monthly Digest of Statistics* and the *Balance of Payments* pink book, identify the data which relate to the UK's international trading performance in the kinds of products covered in Figure 6.3. In the light of this information assess the seriousness of the skills shortage for UK manufacturers.

7

Fixing a deal at Finewood

Figure 7.1

Finewood PLC is a large leading manufacturer of high-quality bedroom and kitchen units. The company has grown to its present size through a process of mergers and takeovers. This integration involved a series of takeovers by which Finewood acquired several companies in the same line of business, as well as suppliers of materials, parts and components. In particular it increased its market share when it merged with a company called Woodway which owned 15 showrooms in town-centre sites.

Despite some rationalization of capacity Finewood still operates factories in Swindon, Oldham, Wembley and Ashford in Kent. These factories not only supply the showrooms but also major department stores throughout the country.

Until recently, it was company policy to negotiate a pay settlement which was awarded throughout the company according to grade and type of job. Under the last agreement, for example, skilled manual workers received an increase of 8 per cent, semi-skilled 6 per cent and unskilled 5 per cent. The various grades of management, administration and clerical staff were awarded increases of between 9 and 6 per cent. Finewood, however, is now seeking to break away from traditional wage-bargaining methods that produce such standard company-wide increases. It is attempting to negotiate settlements on a local basis which are more in keeping with the local labour markets from which employees are recruited.

The company also wishes to introduce an agreement aimed at achieving a greater degree of job flexibility in its workforce. This agreement will involve the removal of demarcation lines between one craft and another, between skilled and unskilled workers, between supervisors and supervised and between staff and shopfloor workers. The company is especially keen to implement working practices whereby production workers, for example, will undertake basic maintenance, such as setting and adjusting, lubricating, cleaning and minor repairs on the machines they operate. It is also hoped to remove barriers between skilled maintenance workers with different crafts by combining jobs that had previously been done by two or more craftsmen with different skills so that a wider range of maintenance and repair work can be carried out by a single worker throughout a particular factory.

Finewood is also seeking a reduction in the number of grades and job titles to simplify the system of pay bargaining. The distinction between supervisors and supervised would also become less rigid, as supervisors will be required to help directly with the work of their teams when the need arises.

Apart from these changes in working practices, Finewood plans to introduce a retraining programme to prepare for the introduction of new plant and equipment which embraces the latest technology and will necessitate changes in working methods.

The company's marketing strategy is partly founded on the launch of a new product line for the kitchen based upon new hi-tech materials and this will involve some employees in a degree of retraining.

Finewood is investing heavily in the Ashford factory to take advantage of the growing number of European orders which followed its successful display at the Milan Furniture Exhibition.

The company estimates that the changes in working practices and methods will lead to the productivity improvements shown in the table.

	Total Workforce	Projected Productivity Increases (%) Year 1	Year 2
Swindon	320	6	9
Oldham	280	5	8
Wembley	226	4	7
Ashford	187	6	15

NB The current rate of inflation is 8 per cent and given a tightening of government economic measures, it is expected to fall back having reached a peak of 9½ per cent. This will still hide, however, the significant differences in the cost of living between different areas. Unemployment is 5.2 per cent and on a downward trend.

ANALYSING BUSINESS SITUATIONS

The unions are demanding an across-the-board increase for manual workers of 12 per cent, while salaried staff are seeking 10 per cent and a 2-hour reduction in their working week.

1. What would be the advantages to Finewood of pay settlements which
(a) more closely reflected local labour market conditions and
(b) which matched or were below the productivity improvements at individual factories?

2. Under what conditions might an unskilled worker at the Ashford factory receive a larger pay increase than a skilled worker at the Oldham factory?

3. In the light of the union's demands, what problems are Finewood likely to encounter in introducing its new pay strategy?

4. What arguments could Finewood use to secure the agreement of its total workforce to its new approach to the determination of pay settlements?

Working for the Japanese

Figure 8.1

WORKING FOR THE JAPANESE: THE MYTHS AND REALITIES

Stephanie Jones looks at 20 originally held beliefs of what it was imagined working for the Japanese would be like

Japanese business in Britain is booming. There are now nearly 200 Japanese banks and securities houses, more than 50 Japanese insurance companies, nearly 50 Japanese trading companies nearly 150 Japanese electrical and electronics businesses, nearly 50 Japanese motor vehicle companies, more than 100 Japanese heavy industries, nearly 20 Japanese construction companies and nearly 100 others producing everything from fire-alarm systems to fishing tackle.

Altogether, they employ more than 30,000 British workers, managers and executives.

In a survey* based on more than 100 interviews with British employees of Japanese companies, interviewees were asked about their first reaction to the possibility of their joining a Japanese company and the views of their friends and families.

Twenty originally held beliefs of what it was imagined working for the Japanese would be like emerged. There was an element of truth in each of them, but many were exaggerated and almost all were grossly over-simplified.

The realities described by the interviewees paint a rather different picture.

'The Japanese always plan for the long-term'

Japanese companies in Britain, although their strategic outlook is longer-term than that of British and other foreign companies, are in reality subject to very real short-term pressures, mainly because Japanese executives seconded from Head Office are posted to the UK for short periods only – usually three to five years – disrupting continuity and emphasising short-term results.

'The Japanese believe in consensus decision-making'

Textbook Japanese management systems always include consensus decision-making (RINGI). But to what extent is this borne out by reality, especially in the British context?

'On the surface, the practice of Japanese management is very consensus-orientated. Japanese managers don't take decisions in isolation. However', explains Ronald Hepburn, head of public relations for Yamaichi International (Europe) Ltd, 'this system is more of a theory than a practice. In reality, decisions are made by certain senior key individuals, rather than emerging from consensus-based discussions.'

'The Japanese believe in life-time employment'

Life-time employment is breaking down in the Japanese manufacturing sector, but the principal company does not lay anyone off. 'Take Toyota, for example', says Mike Simpson of Dodwell and Co. Ltd, a Japan-based subsidiary of Inchcape plc, distributors of Toyotas in the UK and in several other markets. 'They are within a large group, including several major companies in Japan, and have many associated companies and suppliers. If a staff member is surplus to requirements, he will be moved to one of these other companies.'

'The Japanese are very hard-working'

'An advantage of working with Japanese staff is that they are incredibly hard-working and dedicated', maintains Stuart Fletcher, finance and operations director of United Distillers Group (Japan) Ltd. 'However, there is a myth about Japanese efficiency and productivity. When I first arrived at UDG (Japan), there were only two PCs in the office, and all distribution was handled manually by clerks. Many companies here are over-manned and the way in which they do the work is very time-consuming.'

'All major decisions in a Japanese company are made in Tokyo'

In the early days, decision-making emanated entirely from Japan and newly established British branches maintained open telephone lines with head office during crucial meetings. But as more non-Japanese reach senior positions, autonomy is devolved away from Tokyo and subsidiaries are now left to get on with their business, subject to broad guidelines from Tokyo. Many of the most successful Japanese companies, in both manufacturing and financial services, are now seen as multinationals rather than as Japanese corporates.

'The Japanese pay low salaries'

In Japan, high salaries are not earned until a certain level of seniority is reached, and pay for new recruits is low. So 'when Japanese companies first came to the UK', explains Jonathon Baines, an executive search consultant, 'they did not understand the need to pay the going rate. In fact, because they were unknown then, they had to pay over the odds to get good people. Now, with the increasing prestige of Japanese companies in Britain their salaries are no longer exceptionally low or high.'

'All senior positions in Japanese companies are held by Japanese'

When Japanese companies first came to Britain, they sent over Japanese executives with good English and previous international experience; but now, relatively few Japanese businesses are still dependent on Japanese expatriates for all senior positions. Prospects for promotion for British staff, at first seen as non-existent, are now more promising than in American and other European companies.

'Working conditions are often bad in Japanese offices and factories'

In Japan, factories are basic and without frills, and offices are crowded, noisy and hot. The same was true in many Japanese companies in Britain at first, but now conditions are more comparable with British or other foreign companies as Japanese businesses move to new premises to absorb their expansion.

Figure 8.1 (continued)

'The Japanese feel superior and act accordingly'

Sir Peter Parker, chairman of Mitsubishi Electric (UK), explains this belief by suggesting that 'the British attitude to the Japanese hinges on the mystery of their language and resentment at their success'. In terms of the Japanese view of the British, 'ten years ago, the British workforce was seen as unreliable, leisured and disadvantaged. Under professional management by the Japanese, this is no longer the case.'

'The Japanese distrust all foreigners'

The trust of the Japanese is not easy to earn but it can then be preserved and strengthened. Senior British executives are appointed only after long acquaintance, but then they are given great responsibility.

Sir Peter Parker of Mitsubishi Electric and Sir Douglas Vass of Nomura are the only chairmen of Japanese companies in Britain. Both were approached after considerable familiarity with their future Japanese employers.

'It is impossible for a foreigner to communicate effectively with a Japanese'

The complexity and alien nature of the Japanese language inevitably makes communication difficult, but the vast majority of senior British executives with Japanese companies in Britain have achieved a facility of communication with their Japanese colleagues which has surprised them, especially as only a very small minority already knew, or have learned to speak, Japanese.

'A Japanese company dominates the entire life of its staff'

In Japan children study hard under strong parental pressure to enter the best universities, from which they join the best companies. Girls seeking a marriage partner want young men who work for the best companies. 'In Japan your job is a social marker. In the UK, your work is what you do; in Japan your work is who you do it for', explains Stuart Fletcher of United Distillers Group (Japan) Ltd.

'The Japanese are sexist'

The treatment of women in Japan has frequently provoked criticism in the West. Although the typical Japanese housewife has important financial responsibilities (including investing the family income) she is generally confined to the house and plays a very small part in her husband's working life. However, accusations that the Japanese are sexist may no longer be justified, for two reasons.

First, Japanese men tend to treat Western women in the same way that they treat Western men, making little differentiation between the two. Secondly, and more significantly, there is evidence that Japanese women are joining the workforce of Japanese companies in increasingly responsible roles.

'The Japanese never fire their staff'

The attitude of a typical Japanese company to the question of laying off workers is expressed by Akiro Fujii of Mitsubishi Trust and Banking Corporation in Tokyo: 'firing? . . . No we never do this . . . absolutely never. We offer an assurance of security'. Hiroshi Toda of Nomura Securities Co Ltd agrees. 'Here in Tokyo, there is little difference in the treatment and salary of good and bad people. We don't fire staff.'

Their assertions are not strictly true, for two reasons. First, Japanese employees, in Japan as well as in the West, can be moved to another company within the wider group of companies of which their employer is a member; they are not being sacked, but this move can result in severe loss of status, and public recognition that they are not destined for the top. Secondly, in the context of the West, Japanese companies have laid people off, due to economic downturns and perceived indiscipline.

'Japanese companies employ as many Japanese and as few foreigners as possible'

'If we had enough Japanese who spoke good English, then we wouldn't employ any foreigners at all', a senior Japanese at Nomura in London is alleged to have remarked. However, Nomura and many other Japanese companies now have extensive localisation programmes which depend on employing a large number of locals (nearly 90 per cent of over 700, in Nomura's case). Foreigners are employed not only because they are comparatively inexpensive, but because the Japanese recognise that for many tasks, foreigners can be as able, and as dependable as they are.

'There is no reason why a foreigner should be loyal to a Japanese company'

Loyalty to one's company has become a dated concept in the West, cynically seen as indicative of a time-serving, less ambitious person, who has never been offered employment elsewhere. With the increasing prevalence of headhunting, reasons for loyalty to a company are often questioned and found wanting. As a result, many British executives have little loyalty to a British company; why should they have loyalty to a Japanese company?

But the vast majority of British executives contributing to this survey expressed considerable loyalty to Japanese employers, at least for the foreseeable future.

'The Japanese always impose their way of doing things'

To outsiders, the Japanese have a specific and inflexible approach which cannot be adjusted for different conditions; Japanese success in many markets has resulted from their disciplined approach and resistance to other influences. However, in practice, the most successful Japanese companies have combined the best of British with the best of Japanese.

At Iseki UK, a small motor vehicle distributor, 'the company have adopted certain British management methods to comply with UK commercial practice. At first, there were cries of "in Japan we do this . . ." but British staff insisted "Yes, but in Britain we do this . . ." Now, Japanese trainees are sent to learn British management methods.'

'In Japanese companies employees wear uniforms, sing the company song and do exercises in the morning'

The rituals associated with office and factory life in Japan have become part of the popular folklore in the West about Japanese companies wherever they may be. Fuelled by the popular press, the vast majority of those interviewed, when asked about the reactions of family and friends, reported hearing clichés ranging from compulsory communal exercises to canteens serving only rice and raw fish.

In reality, many Japanese companies in Britain are almost indistinguishable from British companies. The staff canteen at Daiwa does, indeed, provide Japanese lunch boxes and hot meals; but these are outnumbered in variety by traditional British fare, such as fish and chips.

In a factory environment, workers usually wear a type of uniform. At Nissan, the only notable difference is that the management wear them too.

'All Japanese are the same'

The racial homogeneity of the Japanese and their perceived lack of individuality has made it difficult for British executives to identify their differences, but many now realise that not only are particular Japanese people quite different in personality and other attributes, but that the corporate culture of different Japanese companies also varies.

*Survey researched to form the basis of a full-length book, *Working for the Japanese: Myths and Realities, British Perceptions*, by Stephanie Jones.

(Adapted from *Management Accounting*, May 1990)

INVESTIGATION OF BUSINESS TERMS

Consensus decision-making involves seeking and valuing the views and opinions of all the members of a business organization (from the managing director to people working on the shop floor) before making any major policy decision.

Multinationals are organizations which own and control producing facilities, such as factories, mines and oil refineries, in more than one country. All considerations relating to the organization's growth, development and survival are based entirely on the interest of the organization itself, national pressures having no influence except that constraints may be imposed on the firm by any country in which it functions.

A social marker may refer to a position, job or ownership of property or a consumer good which confers on its owner a level of social status, standing or position within society.

Headhunting involves a recruitment agency or the personnel department of an organization actively looking at the staff of other organizations with a view to fitting them into positions where they have vacancies. Having identified the staff that they want they will then try through various financial and non-financial inducements to persuade those individuals to leave their present jobs and fill the available vacancy.

Corporate culture refers to a generally accepted set of values and objectives or method of conducting business which characterize a particular business organization.

SHORT-ANSWER QUESTIONS

1. Would consensus decision-making work within the context of the UK economy?
2. What part does strategic planning play in the running of Japanese businesses operating in the UK?
3. Identify the major differences between working for a UK company and a Japanese company operating within the UK.
4. Why would it be more difficult to carry out a 'headhunting' operation in Japan rather than the UK?
5. How do Japanese people classify themselves socially?
6. What is the fundamental difference between the corporate culture of Japanese firms and that of UK PLCs?
7. To what extent is it true to say that there is more security in working for a Japanese rather than a UK company?
8. Would an ambitious British worker employed by a Japanese firm based within the UK be able to fulfil higher ambitions?

ANALYSING BUSINESS SITUATIONS

1. What lessons might UK managers learn from their Japanese counterparts regarding the following:
   (a) recruitment;
   (b) decision-making;
   (c) achieving higher levels of productivity;
   (d) pay negotiations;
   (e) working conditions.
2. Explain why company loyalty tends to be treated with contempt in the West but revered in Japan.
3. Why might the advances made by Japanese multinationals into the West ultimately lead to a breakdown in the traditional Japanese style of management?
4. To what extent do Japanese companies have rather outdated attitudes towards their workforce?
5. Analyse the style of Japanese management of UK subsidiaries.

ACTIVITIES

ROLE PLAY

A Japanese multinational company wishes to recruit UK technician-grade workers for its new car plant in Liverpool.

(a) As a member of the personnel department within the Japanese company, design a suitable application form for the technical vacancies. The form is to act as the basis for an initial screening prior to the interview. It should reflect the type of qualities, attitudes and cultural outlook appropriate for someone who is to be employed by a Japanese company.

(b) Application forms should be exchanged within the class and members should adopt the role of applicants for the technician jobs and then try to complete the form in an appropriate manner.

(c) The class as a whole should then jointly analyse both the effectiveness of the forms and also how they have been completed.

ESSAYS

1. Akio Morita, Chairman of Sony, suggests in his recent book that Japanese workers are treated as 'part of the family' even by large companies. Do you believe that UK industry could benefit from such an approach? (Cambridge, June 1988)
2. How far does the style of leadership adopted by management make any significant difference to the way in which people work? (AEB, June 1988)
3. Are the attempts by Japanese companies to motivate their workers merely gimmicks or are they motivational theories?

9

Newspapers and magazines

Figure 9.1

Reading of national newspapers: by sex and by age, 1988

	Percentage of adults reading each paper in 1988			Percentage of each age group reading each paper in 1988				Readership[1] (millions)		Readers per copy (numbers)
	Males	Females	All adults	15–24	25–44	45–64	65 and over	1971	1988	1988
Daily newspapers										
The Sun	27	23	25	34	25	24	18	8.5	11.3	2.7
Daily Mirror	22	17	19	21	19	21	17	13.8	8.7	2.8
Daily Mail	10	9	10	8	9	11	10	4.8	4.3	2.4
Daily Express	10	9	10	8	8	12	12	9.7	4.3	2.6
Daily Star	9	6	7	10	8	6	4	—	3.3	3.3
The Daily Telegraph	7	5	6	4	5	8	7	3.6	2.7	2.4
The Guardian	4	2	3	3	4	3	1	1.1	1.3	2.9
Today	4	3	3	4	4	3	1	—	1.5	3.3
The Times	3	2	2	2	3	3	2	1.1	1.1	2.5
The Independent	3	2	2	3	3	2	1	—	1.1	2.9
Financial Times	2	1	2	2	2	2	—	0.7	0.8	3.7
Any daily newspaper[2]	70	64	67	68	65	71	64	—	—	—
Sunday Newspapers										
News of the World	30	28	29	38	30	27	21	15.8	13.2	2.5
Sunday Mirror	21	18	20	22	20	20	16	13.5	8.9	3.1
The People	18	16	17	16	17	19	17	14.4	7.8	2.9
Sunday Express	13	12	13	9	10	16	17	10.4	5.7	2.7
The Mail on Sunday	12	12	12	3	14	12	6	—	5.3	2.8
The Sunday Times	9	8	8	9	10	9	4	3.7	3.8	2.8
Sunday Telegraph	6	5	5	4	5	6	6	2.1	2.3	3.3
The Observer	5	4	5	5	6	5	2	2.4	2.1	2.8
Any Sunday Newspaper[3]	74	71	73	73	72	76	69	—	—	—

1 Defined as the average issue readership and represents the number of people who claim to have read or looked at one or more copies of a given publication during a period equal to the interval at which the publication appears.
2 Includes the above newspapers plus *The Daily Record*.
3 Includes the above newspapers plus *The Sunday Post* and *Sunday Mail*.

Source: *National Readership Surveys*, 1971 and 1988, Joint Industry Committee for National Readership Surveys; *Circulation Review*, Audit Bureau of Circulation.

Figure 9.2

Reading of the most popular magazines: by sex and by age, 1988

	Percentage of adults reading each magazine in 1988			Percentage of each age group reading each magazine in 1988				Readership[1] (millions)		Readers per copy (numbers)
	Males	Females	All adults	15–24	25–44	45–64	65 and over	1971	1988	1988
General magazines										
TV Times	19	21	20	22	22	19	18	9.9	9.1	3.0
Radio Times	19	21	20	21	21	19	18	9.5	9.0	2.9
Reader's Digest	14	14	14	9	15	17	14	9.2	6.4	4.0
Smash Hits	3	4	4	14	2	–	–	–	1.7	2.6
Exchange and Mart	5	2	3	5	5	3	1	–	1.6	7.4
What Car	6	1	3	6	4	2	1	–	1.6	11.3
Women's magazines[2]										
Woman's Own	3	17	10	11	11	10	8	7.2	4.6	4.1
Woman	2	13	7	7	9	7	5	8.0	3.3	3.2
Woman's Weekly	2	12	7	4	6	8	10	4.7	3.1	2.5
Best	2	9	6	8	7	5	3	–	2.6	2.2
Prima	1	9	5	7	8	4	2	–	2.5	2.3
Family Circle	2	9	5	4	7	6	3	4.4	2.4	3.4

1 See Figure 9.1 footnote 1.
2 The age analysis for women's magazines includes male readers.

Source: *National Readership Surveys*, 1971 and 1988, Joint Industry Committee for National Readership Surveys; *Circulation Review*, Audit Bureau of Circulation.

Figure 9.3

N.M.E. and Melody Maker readership profiles

	National Profile	N.M.E.	Melody Maker
	%	%	%
Sex			
Men	48	73	72
Women	52	27	28
Age			
15–24	18	63	57
25–34	19	24	20
35–44	17	7	11
45–54	14	2	9
55–64	13	3	2
65 +	20	1	1
Class			
A B	18	27	19
C1	24	32	34
C2	28	25	31
D E	31	17	16
Regions			
Greater London	12	12	20
London & South East	35	36	48
South West & Wales	14	12	9
Midlands	16	16	13
North West	12	11	11
North East & North	14	10	9
Scotland	9	14	11
Total Readership: NRS		644,000	362,000
Total Circulation: ABC		121,001	70,100

Source: NRS – National Readership Survey (JICNARS) – October 1990 to March 1991
ABC – Audit Bureau of Circulations – July –December 1990
Extract from *New Musical Express/Melody Maker* Media Packs.

INVESTIGATION OF BUSINESS TERMS

National profile refers to the proportions of Great Britain's total population who fall into the different categories for sex, age, class and region.

Class as categorized by the Institute of Practitioners in Advertising:
AB Higher and intermediate management, administrative or professional;
CI Supervisory or clerical, and junior management, administrative or professional;
C2 Skilled manual workers;
DE Semi- and un-skilled manual workers, state pensioners or widows (no other earnings), casual or lowest-grade workers.

SHORT-ANSWER QUESTIONS

1. How might an advertising agency make use of the information contained in the tables?
2. How might the information in Figure 9.1 be used by a newspaper company which is about to launch a new daily newspaper?
3. Identify the general magazine in Figure 9.2 which appears to be doing the best.
4. Does Figure 9.2 suggest that there is scope for the launch of a further women's magazine title?
5. What other type of statistical material might have been of value to the *NME*-readership profile?
6. On the basis of the readership survey for the *NME* what type of product or service would be most suitable to be featured in any advertisements?

ANALYSING BUSINESS SITUATIONS

1. On the basis of the information shown in Figure 9.1 does the newspaper industry appear to be in a healthier state in 1988 than it was in 1971?
2. Imagine that you work for an advertising agency and wish to place a number of advertisements in national newspapers. Suggest the paper(s) which would be most appropriate for the following and give reasons in each case.
(a) a Jason Donovan tour of the UK;
(b) a winter skiing holiday;
(c) retirement apartments in Spain;
(d) a new type of car seat for children;
(e) a financial plan to help with private school fees;
(f) a new type of flexible mortgage;
(g) a portable CD-player;
(h) a French cookery book;
(i) GCSE revision notes;
(j) a new variety of rose.

3. You are employed by a market research company which has been asked by *Woman's Weekly* to analyse its position within the market for women's magazines. As part of the analysis you are asked to display the relevant information in Figure 9.2 on a series of pie charts and bar charts indicating the position of *Woman's Weekly* in relation to its immediate rivals. Comment on your results.
4. If the *NME* wished to increase its circulation which part of the market should it target its expansion towards?

ACTIVITIES

INVESTIGATION

Obtain a number of copies of *New Musical Express* and *Smash Hits*. Carefully study the editorial style, format, coverage in terms of articles and the type of music reviewed, and the type of products and services featured in the advertisements.
(a) Highlight the major similarities and differences between the music magazines.
(b) Compare the proportions of men and women who read each of the magazines and comment on your results.
(c) Compare the age-profiles of the respective readerships of the two publications and comment on their significance.
(d) Examine the degree of correlation between the national profiles and *NME* profiles for age, class and region. What is the significance of your findings?
(e) What do all your investigations suggest about:
  (i) the typical *NME* reader;
  (ii) the typical readership of *Smash Hits*?

LOCAL STUDY

Design a suitable questionnaire in order to carry out a survey within your school or college into the reading of *New Musical Express*. Data should be collected relating to sex, age and class (as determined by family background). Compare your results with the national survey and comment on any major differences.

Sports and leisure footwear

Figure 10.1

Sports and Leisure Footwear

For most consumers the distinction between leisure and sports shoes is largely irrelevant. Apart from a consumer who buys with the express wish of using a shoe for a particular sport, most consumers buy 'trainers', ie shoes with flexible uppers with moulded plastic soles. There are two major factors which determine what is bought: price and brand. Branded trainers from the major manufacturers (eg Adidas, Hi-Tec, Reebok) can command a premium over unbranded trainers. For many consumers, especially younger people, the brand rather than the innate characteristics of the shoe is the major selling point.

For the manufacturers, however, the distinction between the sports and leisure sector is crucial. In the competitive sports sector, technology and wearability are the key marketing points of a shoe. In the leisure/fitness sector, fashion trends and colours play a major role in the marketing strategy. In order to be competitive in the leisure sector manufacturers must react to changes in fashion.

The Sports Footwear Market by Usage, 1988

	(% of value)
Casual only	29
Casual and work	16
Mainly sport, some casual	18
Sport only	13
Mainly casual, some sport	24
Total	100

Source: Reebok *More Return for Your Energy*

In terms of the market breakdown by type of shoe, trainers (ie all trainer-type shoes used for jogging, leisure and sports) represent the largest market sector, accounting for almost 70 per cent of value sales.

In 1988, there was a major growth in the trainers market with the rise of the cross-trainer (a trainer which can be used across a range of sports and as streetwear). The major sports footwear companies are now trying to strengthen their position by rapid diversification. Many are looking for ways of developing new areas such as golf and cycling shoes. The specialist areas generally offer high profit margins to the footwear companies and, as the trainers market becomes more competitive, the specialist areas are being targeted for future development.

There has also been considerable development in the indoor sports market which is one of the last sectors not to have been affected by technical innovations.

Table 1
Segments of the Sports Footwear Market by Usage, 1988
(% of value)

Sport/activity	Sports	Casual	Total
Running/jogging	28	72	100
of which:			
serious running	80	20	100
Walking boots	60	40	100
Racket sports:			
tennis	25	75	100
squash	30	70	100
badminton	10	90	100
Aerobics/fitness shoes	22	78	100
Soccer trainers	40	55	100
Soccer boots	100	—	100
Rugby boots	100	—	100
Golf shoes	100	—	100
Basketball shoes	30	70	100

Source: *Retail Business* and trade estimates

Sports footwear is bought predominantly by men. Around 65 per cent of sports footwear purchasers are male. In terms of usage, men are even more important. At least 80 per cent of sports footwear users are male. The difference between use and purchase is due to women buying shoes for men.

The footwear market relies very heavily upon 15 to 24 year old consumers. Almost 50 per cent of sales are to this age group. Also important are children under the age of 15. Footwear purchases also tend to be heavily dependent on the C1/C2 socio-economic groups. The lower middle class and the skilled working class make up just over 60 per cent of purchasers (this group represents only 51 per cent of the population).

The women's and children's markets are showing rapid growth. Around 50 per cent of women buy shoes specifically for women. In the children's market, almost 80 per cent of purchasers said that children had a major influence on the purchase of their shoes.

Table 2
Profile of Sports Footwear Purchasers, 1988

	(%)
By sex:	
male	65
female	35
Total	100
By age:	
15-24	42
25-34	24
35-44	19
45 and over	15
Total	100
Socio-economic group:	
A	2
B	13
C1	32
C2	31
D	14
E	7
Total	100

Source: Reebok *More Return for Your Energy*

Impulse purchases of shoes form a surprisingly high proportion of sales: around 20 per cent. On average purchasers buy new sports shoes every nine months. Research shows that just under one-third of consumers buy a pair of shoes every four to six months and almost 40 per cent every six to twelve months. Around 13 per cent of buyers are very frequent purchasers, buying every one to three months. These are presumably the hard-core serious atheletes.

Five companies/brands stand out in the market as clear brand leaders; Adidas, Hi-Tec, Reebok, Nike, and Puma.

Table 3
Last Brand of Sports Footwear Bought (all outlets), 1988

	(%)
Adidas	20
Hi-Tec	20
Reebok	14
Nike	9
Puma	9
Others	28
Total	100

Source: Reebok *More Return for Your Energy*.

One major brand not shown above is Dunlop. Dunlop has around 9 per cent of the footwear market and is particularly strong in the children's sector.

The five major brands account for over 70 per cent of all sports footwear purchases. In sports shops they have a stronger hold, accounting for over 80 per cent of sales. In the sports shop, Adidas has a 22 per cent share, Reebok 20 per cent and Hi-Tec 18 per cent. Puma and Nike follow with 12 per cent and 9 per cent respectively.

Considering only the market for trainer-type shoes (ie excluding boots and non-trainer shoes), the brand shares are estimated to be as shown in Table 4.

Table 4
Shares of the Sports Trainer Market, 1988

	(% of value)
Hi-Tec	25
Adidas	23
Reebok	12
Nike	10
Other	35
Total	100

Source: *Retail Business* and trade estimates.

Figure 10.1 (continued)

Sports and Leisure Footwear (continued)

Hi-Tec has an increased share of this market with its strength in the serious running market and the leisure market.

Brand loyalty appears very high for the major brands. Surveys show that between 60 and 80 per cent of footwear purchasers would buy the same brand next time. Reebok, Adidas, Hi-Tec and Nike have particularly loyal customers.

Strong brand image has been promoted by successful, targeted advertising. Awareness of sports footwear advertising is high. For Adidas, Reebok and Hi-Tec between 24 and 27 per cent of consumers remembered seeing their advertisement 'recently' in 1988, according to the Reebok survey *More Return for Your Energy*.

Within the individual sports the shares of the companies vary. Reebok is particularly strong in the aerobics/fitness market. Hi-Tec in the squash market, Adidas in the football trainers market and Puma in football boots.

Purchases for children are very important in the footwear market. The journal *Harper's Sports and Leisure* conducted a survey amongst 194 school children aged 11 to 14. The results, which appeared in February 1989, show that amongst this age group Puma has a much higher market position compared with the adult market. Puma accounted for 24 per cent of brands owned and was considered by 29 per cent of the children as their favourite brand. Adidas had the second spot, with 17 per cent of brands owned and rated by 22 per cent of children as their favourite brand. The remaining major companies in terms of brands owned were Nike (13 per cent), Reebok (8 per cent), Hi-Tec (8 per cent) and Dunlop (7 per cent). In terms of favourite brands, these three companies were ranked: Reebok (16 per cent), Nike (13 per cent), Hi-Tec (9 per cent) and Dunlop (2 per cent).

General sports footwear is sold primarily in non-sports specialist outlets, a trend which is tending to increase as fashion/leisure factors become more important in determining sales. Branded sports footwear represents the more specialist and quality end of the market. This is still largely distributed via sports shops. Within this sector the sports multiples are winning share from the independents.

Table 5
Distribution of Sports Footwear, 1989
(%)

	All sports footwear	All branded sports footwear
Independent sports shops	9	40
Multiple sports shops	10	25
Shoe shops	36	10
Department stores	10	10
Other stores	25	5
Mail order	10	10
Total	100	100

Source: *Retail Business* estimates.

The market for sports footwear should continue to grow, with companies broadening their target market away from the 14–25 year olds. The cross trainer has already helped in this move. Women will also be targeted to a higher degree than in the past. There is already a considerable portfolio of female targeted brands on the market and this will be expanded.

Trading up is likely to continue as the technical content of shoes (particularly trainers) increases and consumers become more willing to pay for higher quality brands. The more expensive shoes are also likely to move further into the leisure/fashion market.

In the short term the downturn in consumer expenditure will slow the market, at least in volume terms. Reliance on the 14–25 year olds, although a long term weakness, in the short term has helped the footwear market. This age group is less affected by increased mortgage repayments than older people.

The market for sport/leisure footwear is estimated to reach £650 mn in value by 1992, an increase of 20 per cent compared with 1989, giving an annual average percentage growth of 6.3 per cent over the three years. Bearing in mind inflation forecasts for the period, however, real value gains overall will not be large.

Source: Meal.

Adidas (UK)

Adidas (UK) Ltd is the UK arm of the huge worldwide Adidas Sportsschuhfabriken Adi Dassler Stifung & Co KG. The group is the world's largest sporting goods manufacturer and it produces 280,000 pairs of shoes daily in over 40 countries.

A large degree of the company's success lies with its three stripe logo, which was the first logo to appear on a sports shoe. In 1967 the logo on the shoe was enhanced with the development of the trefoil which is now the Adidas trademark on all leisure goods. The use of the trefoil was a conscious decision aimed at making a visible distinction between leisure products (branded with the trefoil) and serious sports products.

Adidas makes footwear for a wide range of sports, although only about 25 per cent of the company's shoes are used for competitive sports. With around 140 footwear lines, it remains the largest branded sports footwear range in the UK. The company's range of specialist footwear covers 17 sports but its major strength is in the football market.

At least 45 per cent of the company's turnover is estimated to come from footwear, 35 per cent from textiles and the remainder from bags and other specialist products.

Hi-Tec Sports

Hi-Tec sells in 59 countries. It sources its production from overseas (Taiwan, South Korea, Italy, Spain, Portugal and Yugoslavia). Its range covers 28 sports. The company's major strength is in the racket sports sectors.

Hi-Tec has a strong market position in the trainer market because only around 20 per cent of its footwear is used in sport. It still has a market position at the lower end of the price spectrum which is the high volume sector. The company claims, for example, that it has a 40 per cent share of footwear worn casually and 60–65 per cent of running shoes in the £16 to £27 price range.

Reebok

Reebok has been one of the fastest growing sports footwear companies in the UK. A US company, it manufactures most of its footwear in South Korea, plus Indonesia and Taiwan. Its fell running and cricket shoes are made in the UK. The company's distribution policy means that a relatively high share of its footwear is bought for use in sport. The trade estimates that at least 30 per cent of Reebok's sales are for sports purposes. The company's product range is not as wide as those of Adidas or Hi-Tec, but it is particularly strong in the running/jogging and aerobic/fitness markets. The latest developments – a basketball boot called the Pump, in which the lining inflates for perfect fit – is proving extremely popular in the USA and the technology is to be extended to other sports footwear.

Nike

Nike has particular strength in the running shoe market but also manufactures basketball, cycling, football, golf, racket and hiking shoes. The company claims an 80 per cent share of the cross trainer market.

Nike was responsible for the development of the cross trainer, which has widened the footwear market.

Nike is at the top of the market and has benefited from people trading up to higher prices and higher quality shoes.

Despite the expected shifting demographics of the UK population, the company still sees the 14–24 year old as its main target market. One factor in this is that the cross trainer is mobile across age and social groups.

Nike's upmarket image helps explain its relatively high importance in the competitive sports market. Around 30 to 35 per cent of the company's footwear sales are for use in sport.

Puma

Puma has its major strength in the football market. The company is still to a degree football led, with over 50 per cent of sales in this sector (both boots and black trainers). However, the company has extended its product range in recent years into leisurewear. In 1988 around 25 to 30 per cent of its footwear was used for sport.

Dunlop footwear

The Dunlop brand occupies the middle price bracket in the market. The company sells a high volume of shoes at a relatively low unit price. This reflects the company's strong position in the children's market.

Dunlop is very strong in the racket sports markets and offers a wide range of trainers and jogging shoes. It also operates in the fitness shoe sector. The company is also important in the children's football boot market and in the golf shoe market.

Dunlop relies heavily on the leisure sector for its sales. Only around 15–20 per cent of its footwear is acquired for active sports use.

Source: EIU Retail Business, No 385, March 1990

SHORT-ANSWER QUESTIONS

1. What is meant by branded trainers commanding a 'premium over unbranded trainers'?
2. What factors have encouraged rapid diversification by the manufacturers of sports footwear?
3. Why will specialist areas generally offer higher profit margins to the footwear companies?
4. How can a retailer take advantage of the high proportion of sports footwear purchased on impulse?
5. Explain why specialist sports shops account for such a high proportion of the sales of branded sports footwear.
6. What factors could account for Dunlop's particularly strong position in the children's market?
7. Explain why a major manufacturer enjoys a high degree of consumer loyalty.
8. What factors help to make Puma and Adidas particularly popular in the 11-to-14 age-group? Why is Hi-Tec less popular among this group compared with the overall market?
9. What is meant by 'trading up' in relation to sports footwear?

ANALYSING BUSINESS SITUATIONS

1. With the use of an advertisement taken from an appropriate magazine describe the ways in which a manufacturer emphasizes the 'technology and wearability' of a particular type of sports footwear.
2. Explain how fashions in clothing can influence the market for trainers.
3. What are the potential problems that might face a major manufacturer of branded sports footwear if it becomes too closely associated with fashion wear?
4. What factors account for such a large percentage of branded sports footwear being purchased for reasons other than sport?
5. What is the importance of the information in Table 1 to a manufacturer using technical innovation as a means of encouraging consumers to both trade up and to possess a wider range of sports and leisure footwear?
6. Explain how a manufacturer can target its marketing strategy to take advantage of the growth in the market for both women's and children's sports and leisure footwear.
7. What is the significance of the information in Table 2 in relation to the marketing strategy of a sports footwear manufacturer?
8. How could manufacturers respond to the increasing number of people in the older age groups?
9. Assess the likely impact of a period of rising unemployment and higher rates of interest upon the market for different kinds of sports and leisure footwear.
10. Assess the role of products other than footwear in strengthening a company's position in a particular segment of the sports footwear market.
11. Explain the importance of the information relating to frequency of purchase for the marketing strategy of a manufacture.
12. Why do forecasts concerning the growth in the market for sports and leisure footwear have to take account of the rate of inflation?
13. Consider the advantages and disadvantages of a major manufacturer of sports and leisure footwear using its brand name to sell non-sporting goods.
14. Identify and explain the various economic, social and demographic factors which influence the market for sports and leisure footwear.

ACTIVITIES

INVESTIGATION

Select a colour advertisement for a particular brand of sports footwear. Analyse and comment upon the advertisement as part of the manufacturer's marketing strategy. This should include coverage of the following points:

(a) choice of magazine or colour supplement;
(b) timing;
(c) image portrayed by people involved;
(d) setting – foreground and background;
(e) choice of colours and hues;
(f) words used in the advertising copy;
(g) appeal to human emotions, needs, sentiments;
(h) overall impact, e.g. clever, macho, trend-setting, fashionable, innovative, high-tech, sophisticated, graceful, attractive, etc.;
(i) the main selling points of the product.

ESSAY QUESTION

Distinguish between cost-based and market-based pricing methods. Discuss the relative merits of each group of methods and suggest where they would be most appropriately used. (Cambridge, June 1988)

The housing market

Figure 11.1

Causes of the recent house price boom

The sudden acceleration in the rate of house price inflation during 1988 was quite unexpected and many 'post-mortems' have been carried out as to the cause. House prices are determined by the interaction of demand and supply-side forces such as growth in real incomes, the cost and availability of funds, household formation, the rate of new-housebuilding, etc. On the demand-side a major contributory factor was the extensive deregulation of financial services that has been emerging throughout the 1980s, culminating in the Trustee Savings Banks and Building Societies Acts. This has resulted in a massive expansion of credit for all purposes, including house purchase, as lending restrictions have been eased. At the same time, there has been an influx of new players into the mortgage finance market (such as The Mortgage Corporation), adding still further to the growing availability of mortgage funds. Competition in the financial services sector has never been as intense and, coupled with the 'free market' philosophy of the government's supply-side policies, this has resulted in a plethora of financial innovations. At the same time, this competition has encouraged more flexible lending criteria on the part of banks, building societies, insurance companies, etc, as each institution has fought to maintain and increase its share of the market.

However, deregulation cannot be held solely responsible for the magnitude of the 1988 boom. There were three other factors of special importance in 1988 which in total may have had a greater impact or at least may have triggered a sudden surge on the demand-side and which fuelled house prices. These were:

- A relaxed monetary stance at the beginning of 1988 with a sharp decline in interest rates, engineered by the government, as part of an exchange rate policy to maintain a sterling-deutschemark relationship at around 3DM per £. The reduction of interest rates was also motivated by the government's desire to offset deflationary forces that were anticipated as a consequence of the previous October's Stock Market Crash ('Black Monday' of 19 October 1987).

- The announcement by the Chancellor in his 1988 budget of the abolition of multiple mortgage tax relief with effect from 1 August of that year. Under the old scheme tax relief was available on each mortgage loan of up to £30,000 which formed part of any joint house purchase by two or more individuals (other than married partners). After 1 August, tax relief was restricted to £30,000 per dwelling, rather than to individuals. By making the announcement four months in advance this had the effect of creating a stampede for mortgage funds to beat the deadline, particularly at the bottom end of the housing ladder – from first-time buyers. This surge in demand had inevitable consequences for house prices across the whole housing market as activity was stimulated at the bottom end.

- In the same budget, a substantial cut in personal income tax rates, from 60 per cent to 40 per cent at the top end, and from 27 per cent to 25 per cent at the bottom end. This resulted in a sharp increase in real disposable income, further fuelling the already growing demand for house purchase.

There is little doubt also that this growth in real spending power, coupled with cheaper finance, was reinforced by a so-called 'wealth effect'. This wealth effect is associated with the growth in owner-occupation and with the extent to which the value of the owner-occupied stock of houses has more than kept pace with inflation throughout the past two decades or more. The figures show that personal sector gross wealth (including dwellings) more than doubled in real terms over the period 1969–1988; excluding the housing element, however, brings the growth down to an increase of around two thirds. Against this background, people's expectations of prosperity and future affordability of higher mortgages were enhanced still further by the perception of an optimistic economic outlook prevailing in mid-1988.

A slowdown in the housing market was inevitable. The market was bound to lose momentum because of the one-off stimulus injected into it by the budget. At the same time, the government has felt compelled to increase interest rates to their highest level since 1980 and indeed to record levels relative to inflation in an attempt to reduce the over-heating of the economy which has been the primary cause of a mounting balance of trade deficit.

The supply-side of the housing market has responded sharply to the scale of the downturn in demand. Between the last quarter of 1988 and the last quarter of 1989, new private sector housing starts fell by nearly 40 per cent.

At the same time, housebuilders have responded aggressively to the sudden reversal in their fortunes by heavily discounting prices if necessary and by actively introducing a wide range of new financial packages in order to sustain demand as much as possible.

In the meantime, earnings growth has continued to stay ahead of inflation and this, coupled with the decline in real house prices that is now occurring, will help to offset the current depressing influence of high interest rates. All econometric studies show real income to be a major determinant of housing demand and prices.

In the longer term, demand for housing is driven by underlying demographic factors and these remain expansionary for the rest of the century and beyond. Official estimates indicate that the total number of households is expected to go on increasing, averaging 150,000 more per year between 1991 and 1996. While this growth will decline to around 95,000 per year between 1996 and 2001, the total increase in the number of new households is expected to exceed more than 1.2 million in England and Wales alone over the whole of the next decade.

	Housing Starts (Thousands)	Housing Completions (Thousands)	Mortgage Interest Rate %
1980	155.2	235.5	14.95
1981	154.6	199.7	13.65
1982	194.0	175.8	12.91
1983	221.4	199.0	10.62
1984	198.2	209.7	11.38
1985	200.1	196.7	12.64
1986	213.9	205.1	11.91
1987	226.8	211.5	11.56
1988	250.2	225.1	10.97
1989	196.4	201.8	13.61
1988 IV	58.1	58.4	12.72
1989 I	54.7	52.7	13.33
II	57.9	49.0	13.45
III	46.0	48.5	13.49
IV	37.9	51.6	14.18
1990 I	43.0	45.8	14.74
II	42.2	43.5	15.25
III	38.7	45.1	—

Figure 11.1 (cont.)

Annual Percentage Changes in Nominal House Prices Quarter on Quarter 1960 Q1–1990 Q1, UK

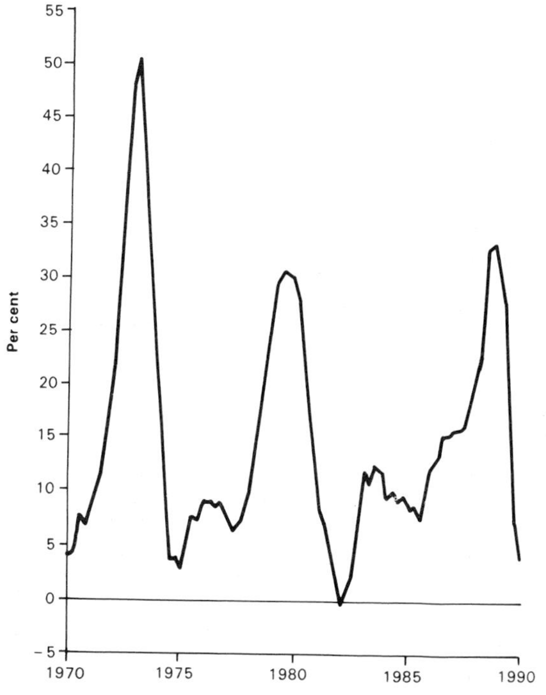

Figure 11.1 (cont.)

HALIFAX STANDARDISED INDICES OF HOUSE PRICES

The Halifax regional house price indices are derived from the Society's large number of mortgage approvals each quarter. These indices which are base weighted take into account changes in the mix of houses between quarters. Technical details are available free on request.

INDEX 1983 = 100

NEW HOUSES

Region		North		Yorkshire & Humberside		North West		East Midlands		West Midlands		East Anglia		South West		South East		Greater London		Wales		Scotland		Northern Ireland		UK		[1]AVERAGE PRICE £
		Index	%	Index	%	Index	%	Index	%	Index	%	Index	%	Index	%	Index	%	Index	%	Index	%	Index	%	Index	%	Index	%	
1983		100.0		100.0		100.0		100.0		100.0		100.0		100.0		100.0		100.0		100.0		100.0		100.0		100.0		34,795
1984		105.2	5.2	106.0	6.0	103.1	3.1	107.5	7.5	105.8	5.8	108.6	8.6	106.7	6.7	109.2	9.2	107.8	7.8	105.5	5.5	106.8	5.8	108.9	8.9	106.9	6.9	34,059
1985		107.4	2.1	111.6	5.3	109.4	6.1	116.3	8.2	110.8	4.7	121.8	12.1	115.3	8.1	122.1	11.9	123.2	14.3	111.4	5.5	113.6	6.4	115.4	5.9	115.4	8.0	37,357
1986		112.2	4.5	116.9	4.7	114.4	4.6	124.7	7.2	119.3	7.7	138.0	13.3	127.3	10.3	141.7	16.1	151.1	22.6	117.7	5.7	120.3	5.9	121.4	5.2	126.6	9.6	44,749
1987		120.0	6.9	125.7	7.5	119.4	4.4	137.4	10.2	129.9	8.9	167.0	21.0	151.5	19.0	172.1	21.4	179.0	18.5	130.6	11.0	129.0	7.2	123.5	1.7	141.9	12.1	54,411
1988		136.6	13.8	145.8	16.1	138.1	15.7	177.6	29.2	170.4	31.2	237.0	41.9	207.3	36.9	224.8	30.6	224.4	25.3	161.1	23.4	138.6	7.4	133.3	7.9	175.4	23.6	67,535
1989		172.3	26.1	196.9	35.0	177.8	28.7	226.7	27.7	220.0	29.1	243.1	2.6	231.5	11.7	236.3	5.1	231.5	3.2	207.5	28.8	154.5	11.5	133.9	4.2	206.2	17.6	73,561
1990		192.5	11.7	210.4	6.9	198.3	11.5	216.8	−4.3	215.3	−2.1	225.2	−7.4	220.5	−4.7	223.6	−5.4	223.9	−3.3	209.1	0.8	168.3	9.0	146.5	5.4	207.8	0.8	77,405
1989	Q4	183.1	18.1	200.2	13.6	188.1	20.5	222.2	−1.3	214.5	−2.4	231.5	−15.5	221.4	−6.9	229.1	−8.0	230.2	−4.7	208.9	8.9	159.3	8.2	133.7	−3.5	205.5	2.2	71,057
1990	Q1	190.8	17.9	208.3	13.0	194.0	15.4	216.7	−2.7	210.2	−9.5	228.1	−15.2	223.3	−5.6	225.1	−9.3	225.9	−3.3	208.9	0.7	164.0	8.5	140.2	2.2	206.6	0.7	75,364
	Q2	193.5	14.5	213.8	7.4	195.7	12.8	218.0	−5.1	224.4	0.5	232.7	−4.4	221.6	−7.7	223.5	−8.1	231.0	−2.4	205.9	0.7	168.4	10.7	149.5	7.7	209.7	0.3	77,958
	Q3	199.5	13.5	211.3	4.9	198.6	11.9	214.1	−6.9	214.0	−1.3	217.7	−9.4	218.0	−5.9	222.6	−3.8	224.2	−1.8	215.7	1.3	173.4	9.6	145.0	2.3	208.2	0.6	79,339
	Q4	**190.4**	**4.0**	**208.1**	**4.0**	**206.2**	**9.6**	**215.9**	**−2.9**	**214.4**	**0.0**	**217.8**	**−5.9**	**215.5**	**−2.7**	**220.9**	**−3.6**	**211.4**	**−8.1**	**208.2**	**−0.3**	**168.3**	**5.6**	**148.7**	**11.2**	**205.7**	**0.1**	**78,013**

Region = Economic Planning Region

% = Percentage change over the same period last year

[1] Arithmetic average of house prices (not standardised)

ALL HOUSES

	UNITED KINGDOM					
	Pre 1919 £	1919–45 £	1946–60 £	Post 1960 Not New £	New £	ALL £
Terraced Houses	47,418	50,441	47,684	53,470	57,711	49,992
Semi-Det Houses	79,857	66,148	56,104	54,994	57,571	62,284
Det Houses	137,544	141,890	130,657	104,808	108,463	115,412
Bungalows	62,214	77,238	76,951	66,833	67,966	70,242
Flats and Maisonettes	56,784	49,452	48,564	47,347	57,352	52,734
ALL	60,760	70,281	66,855	66,139	78,013	66,811

Figure 11.1(b)

House Price-Earnings Ratios 1969–1989

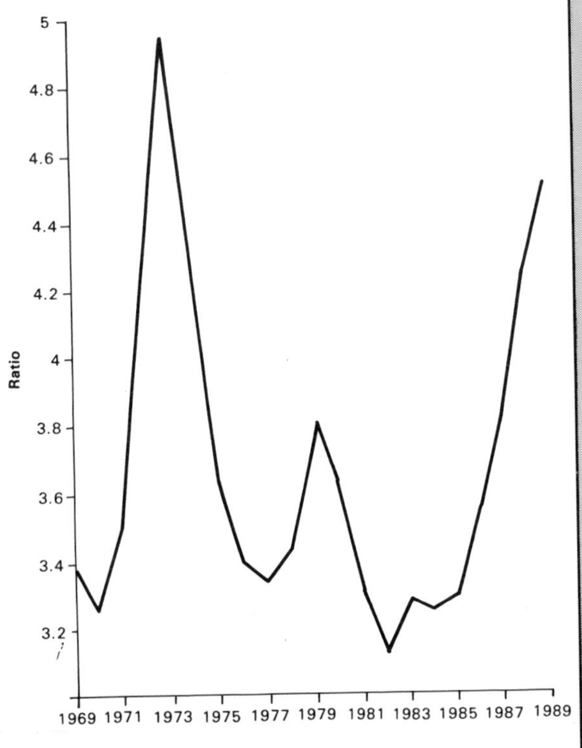

Source: Authors' calculations based on official statistics

Figure 11.1(c)

Initial Mortgage Repayments as a Percentage of Average Earnings, 1969–1989

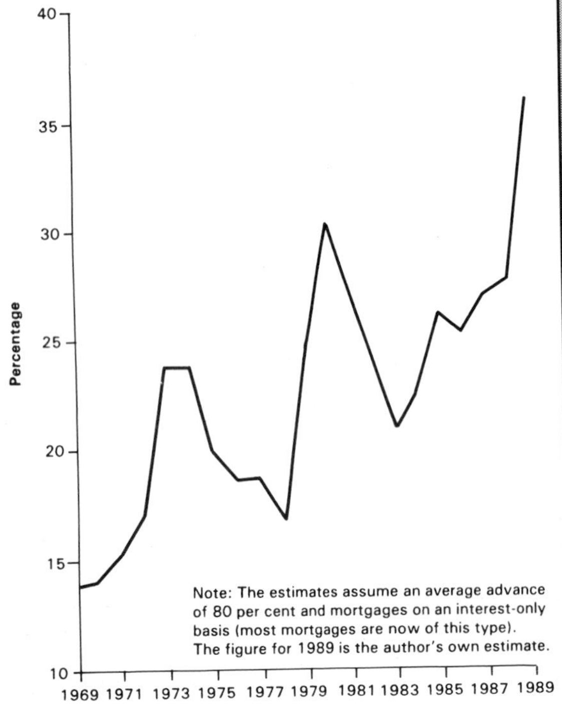

Note: The estimates assume an average advance of 80 per cent and mortgages on an interest-only basis (most mortgages are now of this type). The figure for 1989 is the author's own estimate.

Source: Building Societies Association

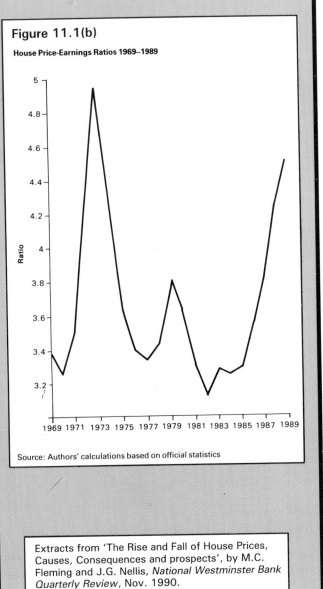

Extracts from 'The Rise and Fall of House Prices, Causes, Consequences and prospects', by M.C. Fleming and J.G. Nellis, *National Westminster Bank Quarterly Review*, Nov. 1990.

SHORT-ANSWER QUESTIONS

1. Why is it necessary to use index numbers when monitoring movements in regional house prices?
2. Why did the deregulation of financial services lead to a greater availability of credit?
3. Why will some people be more inclined to take on a mortgage if it becomes easier to obtain credit to pay for other items such as consumer durables?
4. What developments can lead to the rise in the average level of real disposable income and thus help to stimulate the demand for housing?
5. Why will an increased demand for houses from first-time buyers cause prices to rise across the whole housing market?
6. How will interest rates affect housebuilding costs?

ANALYSING BUSINESS SITUATIONS

1. Describe how regional changes in the prices of new houses are likely to be influenced by variations in factors which affect the demand for housing.
2. To what extent can you identify a 'ripple' effect in relation to the movements in house prices across the UK? What factors could account for any such effect?
3. Why are housebuilders in the UK likely to experience differences in their costs according to the areas where they operate?
4. Give examples of the ways in which a bank or building society, for example, can be more flexible on its lending criteria to households seeking a mortgage advance.
5. Why will a rise in mortgage rates have a major effect upon the level of consumer spending and therefore 'reduce the overheating of the economy'?
6. How do you convert nominal house prices into real house prices? Why will a fall in real house prices help to produce a recovery in the demand for new houses?
7. Explain how expectations concerning future house prices and earnings will encourage first-time buyers in particular to take out as large a mortgage as they can afford.
8. Assume that a couple take out a joint mortgage for £60,000 of the type whereby monthly repayments are accounted for solely by interest payments, the eventual repayment of the capital sum being linked to a life assurance policy.
   (a) Calculate the monthly repayments based upon the following:
      (i) the mortgage interest rate is 12 per cent;
      (ii) the first £30,000 of a mortgage on a dwelling qualifies for tax relief on interest payments;
      (iii) the housebuyer pays income tax only at the standard rate.
   (b) What would have been the monthly repayments if each partner had been able to qualify for the tax relief on £30,000?
   (c) With the help of a numerical example, explain why relatively small changes in interest rates have such a marked effect upon the demand for new houses in particular.

ACTIVITIES

LOCAL STUDY

Using local newspapers and estate agents, collect information on new housing developments in your area. Pay particular attention to the following:

(a) the distribution of the new housing between different price brackets;
(b) the density of housing units on each development;
(c) the types of dwellings, e.g. terraced, semi-detached, flats etc.;
(d) any financial packages offered to make them more affordable, including 'free' extras such as fitted kitchens, appliances and choice of carpets and curtains etc.

Use your findings to comment on how these local housing developments have been affected by such factors as the local employment situation and real disposable incomes, demographic trends, interest rates and local building costs.

Filofax

Figure 12.1

Filofax warns it'll be out of pocket

By Vanessa Houlder

YESTERDAY, IT was Filofax's turn to be the fashion victim.

The personal organiser company, which was once the symbol of upward mobility, saw its value spiral further downwards when it warned it would stay in loss in the second half of 1989.

The shares which were valued at 120p when they floated close to the height of the 1987 bull market, fell 2p to 36p.

Filofax, which blames this latest blow on disappointing Christmas sales, may feel that its problems are no worse than other retailers. However, the company has always attracted attention from the media out of any proportion to its size.

It summed up the aspirations of the 1980s when the pursuit of being conspicuously affluent, busy and trendy merited an ostentatious method of filing addresses, appointments and contacts.

So great was the hype attracted by Filofax that sales rocketed from less than £100,000 in 1980 to more than £12m in 1987. It was an extraordinary new lease of life for a product that had been around for more than 50 years.

But this meteoric growth was a hard act to follow when Filofax joined the market in April 1987. The record of one-product companies – particularly those that could be undermined by cut-price competition or a change in fashion – is not a good one.

Competition duly arrived, and thanks to rivals like WH Smith, Filofax's UK market share has dropped substantially to 55 per cent. Competitors have also blunted overseas sales which account for 46 per cent of the total. In Japan, there are dozens of rival makers of Filofax and price competition is 'horrendous', according to Mr David Collischon, chairman.

Filofaxes have also become increasingly unfashionable as the style gurus of the Sunday supplements shun the ambitious, materialistic values they once so enthusiastically espoused. However, Mr Collischon denies that ambitious, well-heeled careerists are deserting his product. 'All the research shows they are being a bit irritated by being labelled yuppies. But having become a user they become addicted.'

Nonetheless, Filofax has recognised the need to broaden the market. It is now trying to appeal to busy housewives and mothers, who are being courted by a £500,000 'The answer is Filofax' campaign in the popular press.

This flirtation with advertising is a new departure for Filofax.

For years, it could rely on journalists to spread the word. 'We didn't advertise because we didn't need to and we didn't dare. The demand would have been unbearable.' says Mr Collischon. Now however, it has revamped its management team and is taking marketing far more seriously.

Filofax has also tried to diversify.

An experiment with briefcases (known in Filofax-speak as 'paperwork organisation products') has not been totally satisfactory, Mr Collischon admits. 'They are too much at the fashion end. They are not practical enough,' he says. However the Yard-O-Led pens and pencil business is forging ahead, he says.

But the most important diversification comes from publishing increasing number of inserts (ranging from tube maps to GCSE crib sheets) for the personal organisers. Sales of these inserts, which now account for 55 per cent of the total, are 'booming' says Mr Collischon.

Filofax is confident that it will bounce back this year. However, it is not clear that it necessarily sees its future as an independent company. 'We would like to speed the marketing process and that costs money,' says Mr Collischon, who owns 63 per cent of the company. 'If the right sort of partner came along one would have to look seriously at it.'

(*Financial Times*, 13 Feb. 1990)

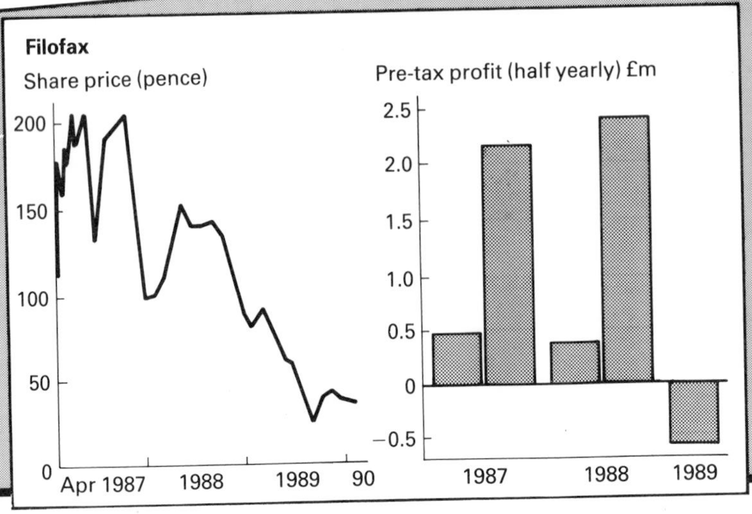

Personal organizer. A comprehensive diary which provides an opportunity for recording, planning and organizing business, personal and domestic engagements, dealings and strategies. It is approximately an A5 size ring-binder usually with a leather or leather-effect cover. The binder allows for new pages to be inserted each year along with other useful inserts which are published from time to time.

Upward mobility. Moving from one socio-economic grouping to a higher one as reflected by type of job.

Floated. Stocks and shares are issued and offered to the general public.

Bull market. Where the buyers of shares dominate over the sellers. This generally exists when people are confident of companies making very good profits.

Conspicuously affluent. Products which are associated with being relatively well-off and in some cases may be purchased by some people to give such an impression.

Hype. Publicity which exaggerates the importance and position of a product in the market, in order to encourage more purchases from those who wish to be fashionable and keep up with the latest trends.

Broaden the market. Developing another market segment for the same product.

Diversify. Increasing the range of products which an organization offers to the market, or widening the variety of existing products.

SHORT-ANSWER QUESTIONS

1. Why might a company be more likely to consider taking over Filofax now rather than in the period immediately after its flotation?
2. Suggest why Filofax's profits were considerably higher in the second half of the financial year.
3. Give other examples that you associate with conspicuous consumption.
4. Give an example of a product where demand has fallen significantly because of a change in fashion.
5. Explain why products like the Filofax are so popular in Japan.
6. Explain what is meant by 'briefcases . . . are too much at the fashion end'.
7. Explain why Filofax published a growing number of inserts.

ANALYSING BUSINESS SITUATIONS

1. Identify the extent to which there will always be a demand for a Filofax-type product. How can Filofax increase the replacement demand for its product? How could Filofax increase the range of its inserts?
2. Account for the success of W H Smith's rival to the Filofax.
3. Explain how the demand for the Filofax may have been influenced by the following:
(a) demographic trends;
(b) the average level of real disposable incomes;
(c) employment in the financial services sector;
(d) image projection;
(e) price competition;
(f) the growing number and variety of domestic arrangements and routines;
(g) the advantages enjoyed by overseas producers of rival products.
4. What would be the advantages to Filofax of greater diversification? Suggest further areas for such diversification and justify your recommendations in relation to products, purchasing, marketing and finance.
5. Describe the main features of the marketing strategy behind the success of Filofax in relation to the four Ps.
6. Assume that Filofax joins up with a manufacturer of stationery products. How would each partner benefit?

13

Launching a new product

Figure 13.1

Mars Press Information

19 February 1990

MARS ICE CREAM BACKGROUND

Since it became nationally available in grocery outlets only eight months ago, MARS ICE CREAM sales have snowballed to make it the fastest selling brand in the take home ice cream market.

Already one in three consumers have tried the product and it is outselling other leading brands by three to one.

The introduction of MARS ICE CREAM was a response by Mars Confectionery to a growing demand in the ice cream market for premium quality brands with universal appeal. British ice creams traditionally used vegetable fats rather than real cream and chocolate flavoured coatings instead of real chocolate.

In a low brand market where products frequently lasted only one season the opportunity to develop consumer loyalty for a strong brand was enormous. Being a seasonal product, ice cream also provided Mars Confectionery with an ideal complement for its confectionery business.

The company began working in 1986 to develop an ice cream bar which retained all the subtle, familiar taste of the MARS bar.

Made with real dairy cream which incorporated the MARS flavour system, MARS ICE CREAM broke new ground with the introduction of a quality dairy ice cream confection for the UK market. It used the same milk chocolate and caramel as MARS but adapted it specially for ice cream temperatures. It also scored a world first with use of 100 per cent real milk chocolate for enrobing, a technique Mars Confectionery had perfected in its role as a confectionery manufacturer.

Following two years of development, the product was ready for test marketing in May 1988 and within a month it had received recognition from the World Frozen Food Congress by winning the top prize for food innovation. The product was such an outstanding success with both the consumer and the trade that in November 1988 Mars committed itself to the construction of Europe's largest ice cream production line – a £20 million investment on a green field site in Steinbourg, France.

By April 1989 the factory was producing for all European markets and in May the product began its national rollout throughout the United Kingdom and across Europe. By September, following an initial national advertising campaign, the MARS ICE CREAM bar had established itself as the number one selling ice cream multi pack. An independent survey showed that nearly 40 per cent of those buying it were new ice cream consumers.

The MARS ICE CREAM single began its national rollout into wholesalers in October 1989.

Since then it has been named best new product in the food sector by the monthly business magazine, *Management Today* and France's most popular grocery magazine, *LSR*, has awarded it the 1989 prize for frozen food innovation.

21 March 1990

NEW GROCERY PACKS BUILD ON MARS ICE CREAM SUCCESS

Following the successful launch last year of ice cream MARS, the concept is to be extended with the introduction of a new range of premium and super premium ice creams for the take-home sector in the grocery trade. Mars Confectionery expects the new range to produce a business worth over £40 million in 1990.

The new products are all built on the personalities of some of the confectionery markets best-known and best-selling brands: SNICKERS, the new name for MARATHON; GALAXY; MILKY WAY; and BOUNTY.

The new products are all aimed at the fast-growing premium sector of the ice cream market. In addition to multi-packs – also growing fast – Mars Confectionery is also introducing its familiar FUN SIZE concept to ice cream.

In the ice cream minis sector, two 15-pack products will be introduced – MILKY WAY MINIS and GALAXY HONDOS.

According to Mars Confectionery's trade relations manager, Lionel Cashin, there is a growing demand in the UK for premium ice cream. 'Mars Confectionery has very strong confectionery brand names which we can use to develop what we believe is an underdeveloped market,' he said. 'Tests indicate that the new lines have the potential to double the level of offtake already achieved by MARS ICE CREAM.'

The launch of the new products is timed to coincide with preparations by retailers for the summer season.

The ice creams will also be available through wholesalers and cash and carries.

8 October 1990

Already 80 per cent of consumers are now aware of MARS ICE CREAM and one in three have already tried it. BOUNTY ICE CREAM, SNICKERS ICE CREAM and the GALAXY DOVEBAR are strong sellers and together have developed sales to £40 million since Easter. As awareness increases, more sales will follow.

To maintain high awareness, we are encouraging retailers to stock and display Mars Confectionery's ice cream range throughout the year. As ice cream loses its traditional seasonality consumers will expect to have all of their favourite brands available all year round,' says Lionel Cashin, trade relations manager for Mars Confectionery. To enable retailers to increase their sales and improve their display of its MARS Ice Cream range, Mars Confectionery has developed highly branded freezers for retailers to purchase. Research indicates that ice cream sales increase when a Mars cabinet is placed alongside other freezer cabinets.

To increase consumer awareness and retail sales of the Mars Ice Cream range through the winter and into next year, Mars Confectionery will be spending nearly £5 million* on new television advertising and promotional support, for each of their ice cream products.

Source: Mars UK Limited.

Figure 13.2

Costly ice cream warfare

The chocolate god of war's new weapon has blown a chill wind through the industry, **Jason Nissé** reports

'THE largest threat to Unilever anywhere in the world today,' is how one Unilever executive recently described Mars ice cream.

The launch of an ice cream version of the eponymous chocolate bar, along with a version of Snickers (née Marathon) and brands such as Bonanza and Milky Way, by Mars Confectionery 10 months ago has shaken up a market dominated by Unilever's Wall's for as long as anyone can remember.

So far this year Mars is the best selling branded ice cream, having sold around £70m in products. That is even more than the mighty Cornetto, Wall's worldwide bestseller. Although Wall's is putting a brave face on it, there are worried expressions at its Walton-on-Thames headquarters.

Mars is attracting two markets: the largest is known in the trade as wrapped impulse. Essentially the customer walks into a confectionery, tobacco and newsagent shop (known as CTN) and buys an iced snack – a lolly, a Cornetto, a King Cone (Lyons Maid) or whatever. In 1989 Wall's had 68.5 per cent of this market, and its pre-eminent position means that many smaller CTNs which do not have room for both a Wall's and Lyons Maid fridge, only stock Wall's.

Mars distribution relies on the Mars ice creams being carried in Lyons Maid fridges. And although Mars has no more than a 2 per cent market share, there is coming a point when many small shops may decide to substitute Lyons Maid fridges for Wall's.

Philip Robinson, general marketing manager of Wall's Ice Cream, discounts this. 'The important thing is to have the ability to offer a range of products,' he says. 'Our share is such that the Wall's fridge will remain the first choice for CTN's.'

The other market Mars attacked was multipacks. Traditionally, supermarket shoppers would buy 10 choc ices for 99p to put in the freezer. Wall's would compete with supermarket own brands.

Mars persuaded shoppers to buy packs of four for £1.99, causing a revolution in the multipack market. In the last year this market has grown by 15 per cent in volume terms and 30 per cent in value. Mars has been able to open up markets Wall's and Lyons Maid had all but despaired of. Consumers are now prepared to pay premium prices for quality ice creams.

Wall's reaction to Mars has been to launch rival products – Bonanza, Sky and Dream. Dream is a joint venture with Cadbury's and is described by Mr Robinson as an ice cream indulgence for chocaholics. Sky is already a pan-European product, being akin to an Aero bar covered in ice cream. (Aero is a Rowntree brand owned by Nestlé. Rowntree's parent, which says it has no plans to enter the British market, but as Nestlé owns large ice cream companies on the continent and in the US, a change of heart is expected).

Wall's claims this trio is not in direct rivalry with Mars. It believes many of the customers who buy Mars ice cream would otherwise buy 'ambient' Mars bars.

Mars does not wholly deny this. It has no direct figures on the substitution of Mars ice cream for Mars bars, but it points out that 40 per cent of Mars ice cream purchases are by people who would buy nothing otherwise, so it is exposing the market. Wall's has taken a stand and undercut Mars by 10p a bar in a bid to steal custom from where consumers can see a price comparison at the CTN or supermarket.

But the empire is rousing itself. A Cadbury's Fruit & Nut ice cream is mooted, as are imports of strong continental products from other Unilever companies such as Ola in Holland.

It may not be as ferocious as the ice cream war in Bill Forsyth's film 'Comfort and Joy', but a war it is – and the shape of ice cream eating in the UK could be undergoing a fundamental change.

(*Independent*, 28 July 1990)

Figure 13.3

Cadbury and Wall's ice Fruit & Nut

Cadbury and Wall's have confirmed that their second joint venture into the adult-oriented ice-cream market is a version of Fruit & Nut as predicted (*Marketing Week*, August 3).

The new product will be available from October, backed with a £1.5m national TV and poster campaign through McCann-Erickson.

Dream Fruit & Nut combines Wall's ice cream with the same chocolate, fruit and nut combination used in Cadbury's £35m a year chocolate bar. The pack features Cadbury's familiar purple livery.

The Cadbury/Wall's alliance launched its first product, Dream, in June following a licensing deal. Wall's claims sales reached a volume of one million in the first week and totalled £4.5m in July.

A second collaboration between the two food companies was immediately mooted, and industry observers now expect a succession of similar products.

The joint venture was spurred by the success of Mars' ice cream version of its Mars Bar, launched in May last year, and now the bestselling ice cream multipack in supermarkets and freezer centres. Mars has subsequently launched versions of its Snickers and Galaxy products.

The UK ice cream market, estimated at £700m in 1990 (Euromonitor) has been boosted by a second unusually hot summer. Recent research by AGB shows that 80 per cent of all adults claim to have bought ice cream in the past year.

But UK per capita consumption is still only seven litres a year, compared with 20.8 litres in the US and manufacturers are expecting further growth during the Nineties.

(*Marketing Week*, 7 Sept. 1990)

* RATE card
MARS Ice Cream Bar, SNICKERS Ice Cream Bar, BOUNTY Ice Cream Bar, MILKY WAY Ice Cream Mini Bars, GALAXY DOVE BAR Ice Cream Bar and GALAXY RONDOS Bite Size Ice Cream Bars are registered trade marks and have been used with permission of Mars UK Limited, the registered owners.

SHORT-ANSWER QUESTIONS

1. What is meant by an ice-cream product with 'universal appeal'?
2. Why have many ice-cream products 'traditionally used vegetable fats and chocolate-flavoured coatings' rather than real cream and chocolate?
3. Why did Mars believe that its method of applying a chocolate coating would give it an advantage over traditional products such as choc ices?
4. Why do you think that the multi-pack was launched before single Mars ice-creams were available?
5. At what parts of the market do you think Mars has aimed its 'fun size' products?
6. What is meant by a 'low-branded market' in relation to ice-cream sales?
7. Why have ice-cream producers been obliged to change regularly their products in order to sustain their sales to children?
8. What factors may have accounted for the success of Mars multi-packs?
9. Why was it only after several months that Mars used wholesalers and cash-and-carries as part of its distribution?
10. Explain what you think would be the most appropriate days and times for advertising Mars ice-cream products on television.

ANALYSING BUSINESS SITUATIONS

1. Why did Mars's branded confectionary products give them an advantage when seeking to develop a market for ice-cream confectionery?
2. Explain why seasonal fluctuations in demand were an important factor in Mars's decision to develop ice-cream confectionery.
3. What kinds of information would Mars have sought to obtain from the test marketing of its first ice-cream product?
4. With the aid of a map, comment upon Mars's choice of Steinbourg in France as a site for its new ice-cream production-line.
5. What are the potential advantages to Mars of introducing their own freezers into CTNs?
6. Why did Mars opt for a distribution system which relied upon Lyons Maid fridges when first launching its ice-cream product onto the market?
7. Why is the question of the substitution of Mars ice-cream for Mars bars an important issue for both Walls and Mars?
8. With the use of some examples, explain why other types of small retail outlets, apart from CTNs, may eventually decide to install a Mars fridge.
9. What are the implications for Lyons Maid of the developing market for premium ice-cream products?
10. Put the case for Mars entering the market for traditional kinds of ice-cream.

ACTIVITIES

INVESTIGATION

1. Investigate the companies and products which are controlled by Nestlé of Switzerland. What factors may put it in a strong position when competing for a share of the expanding market for premium ice-cream products?
2. Identify the various kinds of premium ice-cream confectionery products and design a questionnaire to discover:
(a) the popularity of different brands;
(b) the main characteristics of the market;
(c) the kinds of factors which influence consumer choice.

ESSAYS

1. Filocopy Ltd believes it has identified a market opportunity in a field dominated by one firm – the originator of a novel product. Filocopy have asked you, as marketing consultant, to advise them of actions they should take. (AEB, June 1989)
2. A firm is about to extend its product range. In what circumstances might the firm engage in market research and how might it be undertaken? (AEB, Nov. 1987)

Marks and Spencer

Figure 14.1

HIGHLIGHTS OF THE YEAR

Record sales and profits despite slower economic growth in the UK and overseas.

Capital expenditure of £280 million – financed from the Group's own resources.

New Board appointments and structure reflect planned developments.

Overseas presence gives the Group access to international fashion and design trends.

Investment in information technology and operating systems achieves improved customer service and better sales.

Record sales for St Michael foods underlines customers' confidence in their freshness and safety.

Profits from financial services increase by 45 per cent.

Two edge-of-town stores, five neighbourhood food stores and extensions to our traditional high street locations provided an additional 340,000 square feet in the UK and Eire.

Overseas — new stores opened in Spain, United States, Canada, Hong Kong and Japan.

Major review for UK staff and improved career opportunities ensures continued growth of Marks & Spencer.

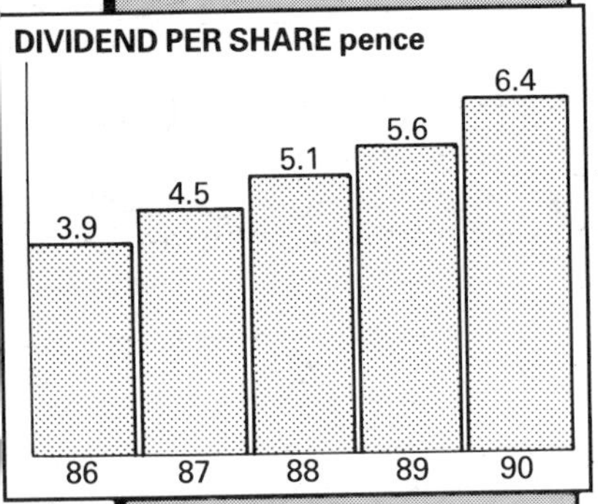

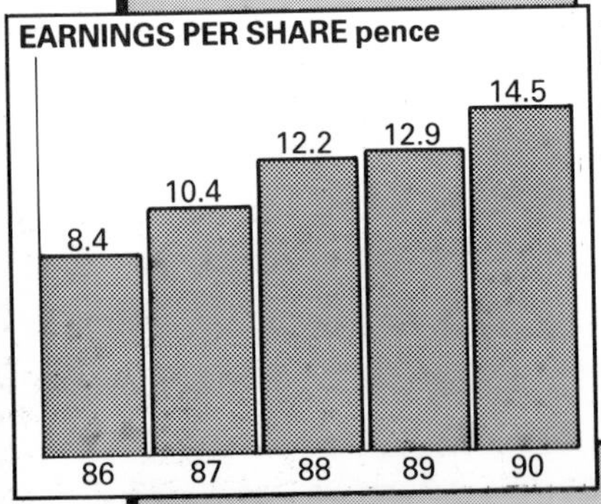

Figure 14.2(a)

FINANCIAL HIGHLIGHTS

GROUP RESULTS FIVE YEAR SUMMARY

	1990 52 weeks	1989 52 weeks	1988 53 weeks	1987 52 weeks	1986 52 weeks
	£m	£m	£m	£m	£m
Turnover (excluding sales taxes)					
Clothing	**2,755.1**	2,522.3	2,249.9	2,118.4	1,866.0
Homeware	**652.3**	611.7	551.6	516.7	439.8
Foods	**2,120.1**	1,923.0	1,730.2	1.549.1	1,410.0
Financial activities	**80.6**	64.5	45.9	36.6	19.0
	5,608.1	5,121.5	4,577.6	4,220.8	3,734.8
Operating profit	**627.7**	563.7	508.5	434.6	361.0
Profit on ordinary activities before tax	**604.2**	529.0	501.7	432.1	365.8
Tax on ordinary activities	**214.5**	185.1	178.4	156.2	141.3
Profit for the financial year	**389.0**	342.9	323.3	276.0	222.4
Shareholders' funds	**2,174.6**	1,918.6	2,158.0	1,578.8	1,452.4
Capital expenditure	**280.0**	209.7	214.5	247.2	163.2

Figure 14.2(b)

FINANCIAL RATIOS FIVE YEAR SUMMARY

Profitability			**1990 52 weeks**	1989 52 weeks	1988 53 weeks	1987 52 weeks	1986 52 weeks
Gross margin	$\frac{\text{Gross profit}}{\text{Turnover}}$	%	**32.8**	32.5	30.9	30.2	28.4
Net margin	$\frac{\text{Operating profit}}{\text{Turnover}}$	%	**11.2**	11.0	11.1	10.3	9.7

Figure 14.3

CONSOLIDATED PROFIT AND LOSS ACCOUNT

FOR THE YEAR ENDED 31 MARCH 1990

	1990 £m	1989 £m
Turnover	5,608.1	5,121.5
Cost of sales	3,768.5	3,458.5
Gross profit	1,839.6	1,663.0
Other expenses	1,211.9	1,099.3
Operating profit	627.7	563.7
Net interest payable	8.8	21.6
Profit on ordinary activities before profit sharing and taxation	618.9	542.1
Profit sharing	14.7	13.1
Profit on ordinary activities after taxation	389.7	343.9
Minority interests	0.7	1.0
Profit for the financial year	389.0	342.9
Dividends		
Preference shares	0.1	0.1
Ordinary shares:		
Interim of 1.85p per share	49.8	45.3
Final of 4.55p per share	122.6	104.3
	172.5	149.7
Undistributed surplus	216.5	193.2
Earnings per share	14.5p	12.9p

Source: Marks and Spencer Plc.

INVESTIGATION OF BUSINESS TERMS

Financial ratios are used to measure the financial performance, prospects or strength of a business organization. The ratios involve making a comparison between one group of financial data and another. They generally relate to particular groups of assets or liabilities of an enterprise and corresponding totals of assets or liabilities; or between assets or liabilities and flows like turnover or revenue.

In the particular case of gross margin and net margin these relate to Marks and Spencer's methods of measuring its relative profitability. Dividend cover provides an indication as to the amount of profit effectively retained within the business.

All financial ratios only provide a meaningful indication as to performance when viewed over a period of time or when compared against the achievement of other similar organizations.

SHORT-ANSWER QUESTIONS

1. Identify two financial factors which have allowed Marks and Spencer to ride out the slow-down in economic growth in the United Kingdom and overseas.
2. What do the financial highlights suggest about Marks and Spencer's long-term prospects?
3. Explain why earnings per share is always greater than dividend per share.
4. What is the fastest-growing area of activity for Marks and Spencer?
5. What factors must be taken into consideration before using financial ratios to analyse company performance?
6. Using the data available, calculate gross margin, net margin and dividend cover for both 1990 and 1989.
7. What do your results in the above indicate about the profitability of Marks and Spencer over the past five years?
8. What would be the best business strategy for Marks and Spencer to adopt over the next five years?

ANALYSING BUSINESS SITUATIONS

You are an employee in Marks and Spencer's personnel department. The company has a general policy of keeping its staff informed as to the financial performance of the business. In order to achieve this objective it is decided that a single-page leaflet should be circulated to all employees summarizing the most important issues included in the Figures.

You are given the task of writing and designing the leaflet. Your departmental head stresses that the leaflet will be read by all grades of employees. Consequently, it should be clearly and simply expressed, technical jargon should be avoided, charts and diagrams used rather than figures and every effort should be made to produce as attractive a leaflet as possible.

The Cromwell

Figure 15.1

The Cromwell

The Cromwell is a purpose-built hotel situated on a five-acre site between Huntingdon and St Ives. It has a total of 75 rooms and is part of the Interegis Hotel Group which has a total of 22 hotels under its control and, between them, these hotels account for 1,400 bedrooms. The attached accounts for the year ended 30 June 1991 have been prepared for incorporation into the group accounts. In preparing these accounts the management have taken the following into consideration.

Depreciation policy
Freehold premises – depreciation of £15,000 per annum commencing from 1 June 1989.
Kitchen equipment – application of the straight-line method of depreciation writing off totally over twenty years.
Furniture and fittings – as for kitchen equipment, except to be written off over 25 years.
China and furnishings – an annual valuation to be maintained at £75,000, all purchases during the year to be written off immediately.

Guest (or bed) capacity
Of the 75 bedrooms available for letting 55 were double rooms and 20 single rooms. This gives a maximum guest (or bed) occupancy for a year of 47,450. In the event of no single room being available a double room would be let at the single rate. The sales figure represents the cost of letting rooms only. The sales value of any meals taken by room occupiers is included in food sales. The actual guest occupancy for the years ended 30 June 1990 and 30 June 1991 was 28,470 and 26,098 respectively.

Food sales
This figure represents meals served to both residents and non-residents in both the restaurant and the coffee shop.

Room lettings
In addition to normal room lettings the hotel offers 'bargain breaks' of two or three nights at greatly reduced prices.

Comparative efficiency with other hotels in the group
The average achievement of the other hotels in the group is represented by the following figures which are constant for 1990 and 1991.

Gross margins:
Food sales: 70%
Liquor sales: 65%
Tobacco sales: 8%
Other sales: 75%
Net profit after tax to sales ratio: 15%
Net profit after tax to capital employed ratio: 10%

Labour cost to sales ratio: 30%
Total overhead cost to sales ratio: 24%
Guest occupancy: 75%
Working capital: 1.6:1
Liquid capital ratio: 1:1
Rate of stock turn: 10 times

Figure 15.2

Revenue account of **The Cromwell** *for year ended 30 June 1991* £

	1991 Sales	1991 Cost of sales	1991 Gross profit	1990 Sales	1990 Cost of sales	1990 Gross profit
Room sales	771,750	—	771,750	735,000	—	735,000
Food sales	924,000	351,120	572,880	840,000	294,000	546,000
Liquor sales	356,160	160,272	195,888	336,000	134,400	201,600
Tobacco sales	138,600	127,512	11,088	126,000	115,920	10,080
Other sales	66,150	23,152	42,998	63,000	18,900	44,100
	2,256,660	662,056	1,594,604	2,100,000	563,220	1,536,780
Less unappropriated costs:						
Wages		693,000			630,000	
Overheads:						
Rates	36,000			30,000		
Maintenance	52,500			45,000		
Depreciation	105,000			105,000		
China and furnishing	37,500			30,000		
Heat, light, power	262,500			225,000		
Laundry	37,500			30,000		
Advertising	18,000			15,000		
Administrative expenses*	33,000			30,000		
Miscellaneous expenses	21,750	603,750	1,296,750	15,000	525,000	1,155,000
Net profit for year			297,854			381,780
Less provision for tax			104,249			133,623
			193,605			248,157
Balance from Profit and Loss account, previous year			205,911			227,754
			399,516			475,911
Less proposed dividends:						
Preference		120,000			120,000	
Ordinary		150,000	270,000		150,000	270,000
			129,516			205,911

* Includes debenture interest

Figure 15.3

Balance sheet of **The Cromwell** *as at 30 June 1991*

£

	1991 Cost	1991 Cumulative depreciation	1991 Book value	1990 Cost	1990 Cumulative depreciation	1990 Book value
Fixed assets						
Freehold premises	2,040,000	30,000	2,010,000	2,040,000	15,000	2,025,000
Kitchen equipment	1,050,000	315,000	735,000	1,050,000	262,500	787,500
Furniture and fittings	937,500	225,000	712,500	937,500	187,500	750,000
China and furnishings	75,000	—	75,000	75,000	—	75,000
	4,102,500	570,000	3,532,500	4,102,500	465,000	3,637,500
Working capital						
Current assets						
Stocks	105,500			83,500		
Debtors	198,000			200,000		
Bank	343,000			345,000		
Cash	749			1,500		
	647,249			630,000		
Less current liabilities						
Creditors	64,395			65,466		
Provision for tax	104,249			133,623		
Provision for dividends:						
Preference shares	120,000			120,000		
Ordinary shares	150,000			150,000		
	438,644		208,605	469,089		160,911
			3,741,105			3,798,411
Financed by:						
Authorised and issued share capital						
1 500 000 ordinary shares of £1			1,500,000			1,500,000
1 200 000 10% preference shares of £1			1,200,000			1,200,000
			2,700,000			2,700,000
Reserves						
General reserves			742,500			742,500
Profit and loss account			129,516			205,911
			3,572,016			3,698,411
8% debentures			150,000			150,000
Capital employed			3,722,016			3,798,411

ANALYSING BUSINESS SITUATIONS

The central management team of the Interegis Group regularly monitors the performance of each individual hotel against that of the group as a whole. Assume that you work in the Financial Department of the Group and you are given the task of:

(a) examining the profitability and financial stability of The Cromwell for the two years for which data are available and comparing these figures with average figures achieved by the group as a whole;

(b) identifying and commenting on why the results may differ between The Cromwell and the Interegis Group as a whole;

(c) commenting on the value and validity of making comparisons between The Cromwell's financial performance and that of the average of the Group overall.

Present your findings in a suitable internal memorandum for the Finance Manager of the Interegis Group.

Computers in manufacturing

Figure 16.1

TAKING STOCK OF THE SYSTEM

By Malcolm Wheatley

An awful lot of manufacturing companies have computer systems these days. An awful lot of these systems were sold on the salesman's promises about the *manufacturing* benefits that the system would deliver. And an awful lot of companies have failed to achieve these benefits. Overdue orders haven't been reduced. Capacity overloads still occur. Customer service hasn't improved and work-in-progress is *still* too high.

But instead of demanding their money back or perhaps even threatening legal action, companies usually just quietly accept the situation.

The reason why companies behave like this is because they feel that *they* are at fault. After all, the hardware works. And the software – apart from the odd bug or two – works. So companies are forced to conclude that the fault lies with them.

So what *does* go wrong? The answer, quite simply, is that too many companies are persuaded to embark on the implementation process without a clear enough idea of the pitfalls en route, or the whereabouts – and desirability – of their ultimate destination.

Manufacturing systems are usually constructed from a series of 'modules', each comprising a stand-alone set of programs designed to perform a given business function. There's the Sales Order Processing module, for example, which handles the 'front end' of sales. There's also the Inventory Control module, which keeps track of the current stock position of everything and tells you when to order more; and there's the Standard Costing module, which ascribes a value to all these widgets and grommets, and so gives you an overall inventory value.

There are also a number of other modules: the Bill of Materials module, which defines the 'parts explosion' that goes to make up each product; the Routing module, which describes the machine-by-machine route through the shopfloor that each part has to follow; and the MRP module itself, which tells you when to order more raw materials and when to launch another works order.

In many companies the order of implementing these modules is often inversely proportional to their value to the business. And it's very common to find companies that never did get round to implementing any manufacturing modules at all.

This is how the benefit gulf occurs. For not only are companies implementing only a fraction of the modules that they have paid for, but the ones that they *are* implementing aren't the ones that deliver the payback. It's quite nice to have computerised invoices; it's even quite helpful to have itemised inventory valuations. But the Sales Order Processing and Accounting modules are essentially *passive*; they *report* rather than *control*.

But the root of the problem lies deeper than the relative ease of implementation. A more fundamental issue is that companies fail to understand, at a sufficiently senior level, exactly what these systems are supposed to achieve. Managements may – laudably enough – talk about 'computerising production control', but then often go on to count as 'hard' benefits only factors such as projected staff reductions. They overlook the fact that, in computerising the process, they are raising the *quality* of the decision-making as well as the speed and ease with which it can be performed. If the system is doing its job properly, then managements can expect to see clear improvements in inventory levels, work-in-progress and overdue orders.

A manufacturing system should deliver *manufacturing* benefits: not just fewer progress chasers or shiny new terminals to gather dust on the production director's desk, but solid improvements in the control that a company has over its manufacturing function. Perhaps the principal such benefit is the optimising of the shortages versus stock-levels equation. Every MRP system can perform this 'MRP I' process, whereby even the most complex assembled products are exploded into their individual parts, and the projected usage of each component determined from the sum of the order book, forecast and spare part demands for the 'top level' product that each part ultimately goes into. These projected demands are then offset against the current stock on hand, together with any outstanding purchase orders, to yield a 'net requirement'. The process is simple enough, and is conceptually little more complex than the manual processes which preceded it. The trick lies in carrying it out for the hundreds of different products and their variants – each with ever changing component structures and purchasing lead times – that today's manufacturers are required to make.

This is where the computer comes into its own. The thousands of repetitive file look-ups, requirement calculations and lead time offsets may take several hours even for a computer to process, but the scale of the task is such that it would be almost impossible to undertake it manually. Stock record accuracy is a leading culprit. If the initial stock level is wrong, then clearly the final net requirement will also be wrong.

Equally common are the problems caused by an out-of-date 'bill of materials' parts explosion. Again, countless companies have found to their cost the consequences of not being disciplined enough in keeping the computer up to date on which particular parts currently go into which products. Left in ignorance of any changes, the system happily goes on piling up stocks of the old parts, leaving the shelves empty of the new parts when the time comes to use them.

Computer based stock control brings a further set of problems. (And the emphasis here is on stock *control* as opposed to stock *recording*: many systems simply tell you how many of an item you happen to have in stock, as opposed to how many you *should* have in stock.) Even with accurate parts explosions and stock balances, computer based stock control frequently fails to deliver the benefits that it should.

Many companies are initially attracted to such systems because they find that the process of calculating usage forecasts and reorder points for each of perhaps thousands of stock lines is too vast a task to be undertaken manually. But in most cases the helping hand that the computer proffers spends all too much time piling surplus stock on the shelves – or too little stock, thus encouraging customers to go to those alternative suppliers who do have some on the shelves.

Despite these problems, requirements planning and stock control are the computerisation of a complex task in basically the same way as it would be done manually. The computer requires relatively little external information in order to undertake the task: a bill of materials, some leadtime information and a few decision rules, all of which would have to be in place anyway if the exercise were to be done manually.

Once companies start to computerise the scheduling of the shop floor, however – as opposed to the ordering of purchased parts and raw materials – the picture changes. For in order that the computer can tell companies what to manufacture and when to manufacture it, companies must first of all tell the computer *how* they manufacture what they manufacture. And while many businesses have found that the task of telling a computer which part goes into which product is achievable, telling the computer how every part is actually made is vastly more complex. This is not just a computerisation of a manual task, but a whole new scheduling activity which requires a detailed data input of the production processes required to make each of many thousands of parts. On which machines are individual parts made? In what order? How long does it take to set up each machine to make a particular part? And how long will it take to machine a batch? In order to take advantage of the scheduling power of their new computer systems, businesses may well have to invest man-years of effort to build these 'routing files', if they are to undertake the detailed shop scheduling that managements intended them to do when they bought them.

Not surprisingly, the construction of the routing file comprises one of the biggest single barriers to getting a system up and running. Few businesses are aware of the problems in advance. For you only need to build a routing file if you haven't already got one, and if you haven't got one, then of course you don't know how difficult it is.

Today's problems *are* soluble. For although their implementations might have run aground, companies should discover that they've hit a sandbank and not a reef. The ship *can* be refloated, the journey *can* be resumed. And who knows? Maybe the crew have learnt a little more about navigation, as well.

(Adapted from *Management Today*, Dec. 1989)

INVESTIGATION OF BUSINESS TERMS

Work-in-progress relates to production that is still in the process of being completed.

Parts explosion is an illustration showing the constituent parts of a particular product.

MRP is at two levels. MRP 1 refers to Material Requirements Planning and involves accurately forecasting the resources necessary to meet future production requirements. If it is to be carried out successfully it should help to minimize stock holdings. MRP 2 relates to Manufacturing Resource Planning and takes a wider approach covering such factors as machine utilization and the deployment of labour.

Purchasing 'lead time' refers to the time that elapses between an order being placed and the supplier delivering the goods.

SHORT-ANSWER QUESTIONS

1. What are the particular problems associated with computer-based stock-control systems?

2. What 'human' failings may render a computerized manufacturing system inefficient?

3. Explain how a computerized manufacturing system may raise customer satisfaction.

4. Why is the computerization of the shop-floor so much more complex than the ordering of purchased parts or raw materials?

5. Identify what the computerized system can do that the manual system cannot.

ANALYSING BUSINESS SITUATIONS

1. To what extent is the failure of many manufacturing companies to make proper use of computerized systems due to their own inability or the misrepresentation of the merits of those systems by the company supplying them?

2. Outline the major benefits that a computerized manufacturing system ought to deliver.

3. Explain why many manufacturing companies never get beyond implementing the essentially 'passive' manufacturing systems modules.

4. How should the quality of decision-making be raised by a properly implemented computerized manufacturing system?

5. Discuss the view that only an efficiently organized company will be capable of fully realizing the benefits from a computerized manufacturing system.

ACTIVITIES

LOCAL STUDY

(a) Design a suitable questionnaire in order to conduct a survey amongst a number of small local engineering firms into the use they are making of computer-aided manufacturing systems.

(b) Do your results support the arguments put forward in Malcolm Wheatley's article?

ROLE PLAY

Imagine that you work for a firm of management consultants. The consultancy has been called in by a company that manufactures components for the car industry. It wants the consultancy to advise on the merits of introducing a totally computerized manufacturing system.

As a prelude to the full analysis write a letter to the production manager of the manufacturing firm. The purpose of the letter is to outline the advantages of a computerized system, while at the same time warning of the possible pitfalls if it is not correctly implemented.

ESSAYS

1. Why might an organization experience a reduction in profitability following the introduction of information technology? (AEB, June 1988)

2. Discuss the ways in which a firm might respond to today's ever-increasing rate of technological change. (AEB, Nov. 1987)

3. Discuss the view that a computerized manufacturing system may prove to be too sophisticated for some companies to introduce.

Industrial tribunals

Figure 17.1

The tribunals

Industrial tribunals are independent judicial bodies. They have permanent offices in the larger centres of population and sit in most parts of the country. Each has a legally qualified chairman, appointed by the Lord Chancellor in England and Wales, and in Scotland by the Lord President. The other two menbers are drawn from two panels of members appointed by the Secretary of State for Employment, one after consultation with employees' organizations and one after consultation with employers' organizations.

Matters which a tribunal can consider

Industrial tribunals may be asked to decide questions relating to many different matters. The main ones are listed in the following table.

Equal pay

Right to receive the same pay and other terms of employment as an employee of the opposite sex working for the same or an associated employer if engaged on like work, work related as equivalent under job evaluation or work of equal value.

Guarantee payments

Right to receive guarantee pay from employers during lay-offs.

Insolvency of employer

Right to be paid by the Secretary of State certain debts owed by an insolvent employer.

Right to be paid by the Secretary of State occupational pension scheme contributions owing on behalf of employees of insolvent employers.

Maternity rights

Right not to be unfairly dismissed for reasons connected with pregnancy.

Right to be paid time off work for ante-natal care.

Right to return to work following absence because of maternity.

Right to receive maternity pay.

Right to receive maternity pay rebate, and questions relating to the amount of such payments.

Medical suspension

Right not to be unfairly dismissed on suspension on medical grounds relating to health and safety regulations.

Right to receive pay on suspension on medical grounds.

Occupational pension schemes

Right of recognised independent trade unions to be consulted about an employer's notice of application for a contracting-out certificate relating to an occupational pension scheme, including any question about whether a union is independent or recognized to any extent for collective bargaining purposes.

Race relations

Right not to be discriminated against in the employment, training and related fields on grounds of colour, race, nationality or ethnic or national origins, or victimised, for example, for pursuing rights under the Act.

Redundancy

Right of a recognised independent trade union to be consulted by the employer about proposed redundancies.

Right to receive payment under a protective award made by an industrial tribunal.

Right of an employer to appeal against the reduction of redundancy payment rebate for failure to notify proposed redundancies.

Right to receive redundancy payment or rebate, and questions relating to the amount of such payments.

Sex discrimination

Right not to be discriminated against in employment, training and related fields on the grounds of sex or marriage, or victimised, for example for pursuing rights under this Act or the Equal Pay Act 1970.

Unfair dismissal

Right not to be unfairly dismissed.

Written reasons for dismissal

Right to receive a written statement of reasons for dismissal.

Written statement of main terms and conditions of employment

Right to receive a written statement of terms of employment or any alteration to them with sufficient details to meet the requirements of the Act.

Deductions from wages

Right of all workers not to have deductions made from their wages (or be required to make payments to their employers), unless allowed by statute, by the contract of employment or with the worker's prior written agreement.

Additional rights for workers in retail employment who suffer deductions from wages (or are required to make payments) because of cash shortages or stock losses.

Trade union membership/non-membership rights

Right to be paid time off for trade union duties; right to time off for trade union activities.

Right not to suffer action short of dismissal for trade union membership or activities.

Right not to suffer action short of dismissal to compel union membership – whether in or outside a closed shop.

Right not to suffer action short of dismissal to compel payments in lieu of union membership.

Right not to be unfairly dismissed for trade union membership or activities.

Right not to be unfairly dismissed for non-membership of a union whether in or outside a closed shop.

Right not to be unfairly dismissed for not making payments in lieu of union membership.

Right not to be chosen for redundancy because of trade union membership or activities or non-membership of a trade union whether inside or outside a closed shop.

Application for interim relief (that is, re-employment or continuation of contract of employment) from an employee who complains to an industrial tribunal that he or she has been unfairly dismissed for non-membership of a union or for trade union membership or activities.

Right not to be unreasonably excluded or expelled from a union in a closed shop.

Right of union to hold secret ballots on employer's premises.

Transfer of undertakings

Right of union to be informed and consulted about the transfer of an undertaking to a new employer.

Right not to be dismissed on the transfer of an undertaking to a new employer except for certain reasons.

(Adapted from *Industrial Tribunals Procedure*, ITLI (1989), Centre Office of Industrial Tribunals)

Figure 17.2

Monica Davies and the Wilburyshire Ambulance Service

Case Study

Monica Davies was born on 8 July 1943. On leaving school she went into nursing and became a qualified State Enrolled Nurse specialising in work with patients suffering with heart complaints. She left nursing in 1968 to start a family. Ten years later, following a modular training course at Westbury, she qualified in ambulance work and started work on 1 September 1978. Monica was one of two women employed at the Wilbury ambulance station, together with 14 men. The station officer was a Geoffrey Dack who had been in the service for over 25 years. Tim Day acted as the divisional officer and Mike Wilson was the chief officer for Wilburyshire. Monica got on very well with her colleagues and was respected for the cool way in which she handled emergencies. On a number of occasions during the years of her service she had 'acted up', in the sense that she had assumed higher responsibilities when senior staff on the grade above her were away.

In 1987 she undertook a course which led to the award of a paramedic qualification which is normally held by more senior members of the ambulance staff. In March 1989 she applied with Jim Dale and Bob Maxwell for an upgrading to leading ambulance person. Neither of these two men had the paramedic qualification and had both entered the ambulance service in 1983. All three candidates were interviewed for the post, which was eventually given to Bob Maxwell. Monica was disappointed and was told that she had not sold herself very well at the interview or on the application form.

Monica made a further application for promotion in October 1989. She was not short-listed for interview, but was told to keep trying.

Finally in February 1990 two vacancies came up for a leading ambulance man or woman at Wilbury Ambulance Station. Monica was particularly interested in securing one of the jobs because she was finding it difficult to make ends meet on her basic pay of £185 for a 39-hour week, plus an average £20 per week overtime. Monica put in an application and was not short-listed for interview. When she approached Geoffrey Dack, the station officer, over the matter he merely stated that 'He [Tim Day] does not think that you are up to it'.

Monica wrote to Tim Day asking why she was not considered to be capable of doing the job. He didn't reply. Monica rang him three times and eventually got through to be told there had been a lot of applicants and they could not short-list everybody. Monica asked how they short-listed and he said, 'According to length of service, qualifications, sick record and the completion of the application form.'

Two weeks later, Geoffrey Dack called her into his office saying that he wanted to explain why she was not having much success in her application for promotion. He said, 'We don't doubt your ability to do the leading hands job but we don't think you can take the hassle from the men.'

Monica said that she felt quite capable of dealing with the men and was going to take the matter further as she did not feel she was being given the real reason for her lack of success.

Monica contacted the National Union of Public Employees which represents the interests of ambulance women. Mrs Angela Scott, the Union's legal expert, advised her to take her complaint to the Industrial Tribunal.

ANALYSING BUSINESS SITUATIONS

1. Adopt the role of Monica Davies and complete all the relevant sections of a photocopy of the application form, shown on page 42. Pay particular attention to section 10 which should clearly describe how you feel the law has been breached.

You may invent any personal details which are not included in the case-study material.

2. What do you think would be the outcome of the Industrial Tribunal?

17

FOR OFFICIAL USE ONLY

Received at COIT	Case No.	Code
	Initials	ROIT

Application to an Industrial Tribunal

Please read the notes opposite before filling in this form.

1 Say what type of complaint(s) you want the tribunal to decide *(see note opposite).*

2 Give your name and address etc. in CAPITALS *(see note opposite).*

Mr/Mrs
Miss/Ms

Address

Telephone

Date of birth

3 Please give the name and address of your representative, if you have one.

Name

Address

Telephone

4 Give the name and address of the employer, person or body (the respondent) you are complaining about *(see note opposite).*

Name

Address

Telephone

Give the place where you worked or applied for work, if different from above.

Name

Address

Telephone

5 Please say what job you did for the employer (or what job you applied for). If this does not apply, please say what your connection was with the employer.

IT 1 and IT 1(Scot) (Revised July 1987)

Please continue overleaf

6 Please give the number of normal basic hours you worked per week.

Hours [ ] per week

7 Basic wage / salary £ [ ] per [ ]

Average take home pay £ [ ] per [ ]

Other bonuses / benefits £ [ ] per [ ]

8 Please give the dates of your employment *(if applicable)*

Began on [ ]

Ended on [ ]

9 If your complaint is **not** about dismissal, please give the date when the action you are complaining about took place (or the date when you first knew about it).

Date [ ]

10 Give the full details of your complaint *(see note opposite).*

11 Unfair dismissal claimants only (Please tick a box to show what you would want if you win your case).

☐ Reinstatement: to carry on working in your old job as before

☐ Re-engagement: to start another job, or a new contract, with your old employer

Orders for reinstatement or re-engagement normally include an award of compensation for loss of earnings.

☐ Compensation only: to get an award of money

You can change your mind later. The Tribunal will take your preference into account, but will not be bound by it.

Signature: Date:

Industry and the environment

Figure 18.1

BACKYARD

Power of the individual to act responsibly

Rethinking your daily habits can slow down global warming, says **Jeremy Leggett.**

'THE EARTH is slowly dying, and the inconceivable – the end of life itself – is actually becoming conceivable. We human beings ourselves have become a threat to our planet.' Thus Queen Beatrice of the Netherlands, in her Christmas message last year.

Nearer home, the Commons Energy Committee's Conservative chairman, Sir Ian Lloyd, sat through exhaustive hearings on the greenhouse effect and concluded: 'We have, at the most, a quarter of a century to take action. The life of the planet may be at stake.'

But while the broad outline of what actions governments need to take is clear – for a start, legislate to cut carbon dioxide emissions, promote public transport, encourage energy efficiency and invest in renewable forms of energy production – the extent to which concerned individuals can help to alleviate the crisis is not.

Many feel hopeless; they can do so little it is not worth making a start.

Nothing could be further from the truth. There is a wide range of individual 'anti-greenhouse' actions which, taken by everybody, would have a huge collective impact.

Imagine a typical winter Saturday. We wake and turn on the light. Most electricity is generated by burning coal and oil, which emit carbon dioxide. The common light bulb is an incandescent one, which uses 80 per cent more electricity than the less common compact fluorescents. As with most anti-greenhouse actions, we also end up paying less – in this case, on the electricity bill.

We stumble to the kitchen to make breakfast. Here is a most fruitful area for carbon dioxide savings. The energy efficiency of kitchen appliances never features in advertising, yet different brands vary appreciably in the amount they consume. The average electricity consumption of a freezer in the UK is 750 kilowatt-hours per year. The best available freezer consumes only 140kw. Huge savings can also be made on fridges, kettles – indeed most appliances except the kitchen sink. As appliances wear out, anti-greenhouse citizens should ask about the energy-efficiency of products and buy accordingly.

With Saturday breakfast under way, the central heating is likely to have been on for some time. But how much waste will have been involved in heating the air around and above the house? Insulation of lofts, cavity walls and water tanks, fitting double-glazing and draught-stripping to doors and windows can all reduce appreciably the amount of energy consumed in heating a house. In Milton Keynes, where building regulations encourage such developments, electricity bills are 40 per cent lower than the national average. In Finland, electricity bills can be as low as £20 per year in super-insulated houses, despite freezing weather.

We read our newspaper as we unwrap our breakfast cereal from layers of paper packaging. In most households, all this will go in the bin, to find its way eventually into a landfill dump. There it will decompose, producing methane – a greenhouse gas 25 times more effective than carbon dioxide at trapping atmospheric heat.

The atmosphere's methane content is growing at 1 per cent a year. A good proportion of it – tens of millions of tonnes annually – is seeping from rubbish tips. So greenhouse-conscious citizens recycle their paper and do not bother with packaging in the first place. Many health and wholefood stores will pour cereals direct into re-usable bags.

Next stop is the shops. Most people go by car. The average car produces nearly four times its body weight in carbon dioxide each year.

In the UK, our cars manage an average of 30 miles to the gallon. The best available model does 57 mpg. Many current prototypes can achieve between 70 and 100 mpg – one Renault has achieved 124 mpg in trials. Anti-greenhouse citizens will choose their next model with these figures in mind.

They will also share their cars more and use public transport where possible. Some 15 per cent of global carbon dioxide emissions come from cars and light vans. The scope for savings is phenomenal. If the United States increased the fuel efficiency of its average vehicle from 17 to 30 mpg, it would not need to import oil.

Anti-greenhouse citizens will be keen to own a car with a catalytic converter. As well as carbon dioxide, exhaust gases contain carbon monoxide, unburned hydrocarbons and nitrogen oxides. Reactions between the latter two and sunlight produce ozone, a protector against ultraviolet radiation in the upper atmosphere, but a greenhouse gas in the lower atmosphere. All this can be reduced (along with the contribution nitrogen oxides make to acid rain) by catalytic converters.

Once at the shops, our anti-greenhouse choices are legion. We begin by eschewing all aerosols propelled by chlorofluorocarbons. CFCs are 100,000 times worse as greenhouse gases than carbon dioxide and they also attack the protective ozone layer.

We studiously avoid any product made of tropical hardwood, and look for the Friends of the Earth 'good wood' seal. This is a small but vital step in preserving rain forests, whose destruction contributes up to 40 per cent of all carbon dioxide emissions.

Organic food is greenhouse-friendly. Nitrous oxide, a gas produced when fertilisers are added to the soil, is a greenhouse gas. The more people who buy organic food, the more the prices will be reduced and the more organic farming – anti-greenhouse farming – will be encouraged.

Next stop, the meat counter. The world's cattle produce about 100 million tonnes of methane each year. There is roughly one head of cattle for every four humans. Sheep and goats, also ruminants, have the same effect. All add significantly to the alarming escalation of methane in the atmosphere. Anti-greenhouse citizens should eat far less meat.

From here, anti-greenhouse opportunities for the individual move from consumerism to activism. No one worried about global warming should underestimate the power of the post. Lobby your local council for recycling schemes. Get them to plant trees and tap the methane from dumps to heat buildings. Co-ordinated lobbying of businesses, seeking proof of anti-greenhouse production *processes*, as well as greenhouse-friendly products, will surely have an effect on corporate planning.

Dr Jeremy Leggett is director of science at Greenpeace UK.

(*Observer*, 24 Sept. 1989)

Figure 18.2

GREEN LABELLING

WITH THE increasing concern about the environment, more and more manufacturers are claiming that their goods are 'green'. But how justifiable are those claims?

We interviewed 1,930 people last September to find out how much notice they take of 'green' labels, and what they understood by them. We discovered that:

- around 60 per cent of shoppers had seen products with environmental labels in the shops. Of these, nearly 60 per cent had bought at least one such product on their last shopping trip.
- 55 per cent of shoppers shown a label making environmental claims thought it had been officially approved. When asked who they thought had approved it, the most popular guess was the Government (44 per cent).
- of those who correctly thought that goods carrying 'green' labels don't require official approval, 83 per cent thought they *should* require it. Nearly 60 per cent of the people we asked thought the Government would be the appropriate body to give such approval.

We also carried out a series of group discussions with people responsible for doing the shopping for their household. There was a general feeling that some manufacturers are simply jumping on the bandwagon, and using 'green' labels as a marketing ploy. When we considered a number of specific 'green' labels, we discovered that people are confused about what individual terms mean, and suspicious that the claims may be unjustified.

Below (p. 46) we look at a selection of the 'green' labels in the shops at a the time of our research. Some of the labels will have changed by the time you read this report. And not all the labels we found were misleading or confusing. But those we show highlight some typical problems.

Excessive claims

No manufactured product can fail to have some sort of negative impact on the environment. Labels which claim that a product is 'environmentally friendly' are misleading. For example, even if the trees used to make paper products like sanitary towels are from a properly managed forest, pulp and paper production are highly energy intensive processes. Aerosol manufacturers may avoid using the most harmful CFCs as a propellant, but the alternatives can still damage the atmosphere. As for batteries, even those which don't contain the poisonous metals mercury and cadmium are a very inefficient way to use energy – it's estimated that manufacturing batteries take up to 50 times more energy than the amount they produce.

Our view We think that very general labels like 'environmentally friendly' and 'green' should be banned.

Multiple claims

When we looked at the labels on aerosol cans, we found at least ten different forms of wording relating to CFCs and the ozone layer. Yet all these aerosols are similar in that they don't contain the most harmful types of CFC gas as a propellant. The alternative propellants they use may vary (most use hydrocarbons, while a few use less harmful CFCs, neither of which causes environmental problems on the same scale as the most harmful CFCs) but the different forms of wording do not reflect differences in the propellant. For example, there was a general feeling in our discussion groups that an aerosol labelled 'ozone safe' was somehow 'greener' than one labelled 'ozone friendly'. In fact both contained hydrocarbons as a propellant.

Our view Where products are making essentially the same environmental claim, standard wording should be used to avoid unnecessary confusion.

Claims which aren't explained

When we showed these labels in our discussion groups, they weren't thought helpful. Most people didn't know what 'no phosphates', 'no NTA', 'no enzymes' or 'no optical brighteners' meant.

The term 'biodegradable' was not fully understood, nor was the meaning behind the words 'environment friendly pulp'. None of the packets gave a proper explanation of what was meant by these claims, so it was difficult for shoppers to assess how important they were in environmental terms.

Of course, it's best if the information given can be reasonably short and simple. We showed our discussion groups a packet of washing powder which gave very lengthy explanations of terms like phosphates and what they could do to the environment. The groups thought that they wouldn't have time to read this amount of information while they were shopping. But at least they would have the option of reading it.

Our view Information shouldn't be so sparse that customers cannot make an informed choice about what they are buying.

Meaningless Claims

'CONTAINS NO PHOSPHATES NITRATES OR AMMONIA'

It's misleading to put a 'no nitrates' label on a bathroom cleaner, when you can't buy one which *does* contain nitrates.

'PH NEUTRAL, PHOSPHATE-FREE'

Similarly, a 'phosphate free' label on a bottle of washing-up liquid suggests that other washing-up liquids do contain phosphates, so this brand is environmentally better. But *no* washing-up liquids on sale in the UK contain phosphates.

'BIODEGRADABLE'

Likewise, *all* detergents are biodegradable to a large extent since the surfactants (the main cleaning agents) have to be at least 80 per cent biodegradable by law. Products where the surfactants are based on vegetable oils rather than petrochemicals may biodegrade more quickly and thoroughly, but the environmental benefits of this are still unclear.

Our view We think claims like these should be allowed only when an alternative product does have the offending ingredient or property.

Unrealistic claims

It's helpful for a manufacturer to point out what packaging is made of and state if it is recyclable. At present, though, plastic recycling schemes and collection points are few and far between. Consumers may be persuaded into buying a product partly because it has a 'recyclable' label on the plastic container, but when it comes to disposing of it, there is no local recycling point so it just joins the rest of the rubbish heap. On the other hand, if labelling containers in this way encourages people to think about recycling, it may lead to more schemes being set up.

Our view It's up to consumers to be wary of claims like this – and to campaign for more local recycling schemes.

Figure 18.3

THE WAY FORWARD

AT PRESENT there are no official guidelines over how 'green' labels are used. Our survey shows overwhelming support for some sort of official scheme and a strong feeling that the Government should be the body responsible for overseeing it.

The Government have in fact recently announced their support for the creation of an official labelling scheme across the European Community. We welcome this, and have responded to a Government discussion paper on the subject. If all goes well, there could be EC agreement on a scheme by the end of this year.

It is proposed that products would be awarded an official environmental label after scrutiny by an independent panel of environment 'judges'. These would include representatives from consumer groups, manufacturers and retailers. The scheme would be voluntary, so manufacturers wouldn't be compelled to submit their products to the panel, but the right to use an official 'green' label would be a strong marketing incentive.

We do have reservations about some of the Government's suggestions for how the scheme might work. The major ones are:

Assessing only part of the life cycle. The Government has suggested that the scheme should take account of a product's environmental impact only during its use and disposal. So a product might be awarded an official label on the grounds that it doesn't put polluting chemicals into the atmosphere while it is being used and is fully biodegradable once it's been disposed of. But it could still have an unnecessarily harmful impact on the environment during the production, packaging and distribution processes. For example, it could be made of tropical hardwood from an unsustainable source. We think that as many aspects as possible of a product's life cycle, from production through to disposal, should be taken into account in any environmental labelling scheme.

The pass/fail approach. There is a risk that a simple pass/fail system which awards each label for a minimum period of three years could fail to keep pace with technological innovations in industry. A possible alternative could be a graded system rather like we use for tested products in *Which?* magazine. For example, a product which has basic but significant environmental qualities would be awarded one star, another product of the same type that had further environmental improvements would be awarded two stars, and so on. The appropriate stars would appear on the official label and you would be able to see at a glance how different products compare with each other.

SCHEMES IN OTHER COUNTRIES

Environmental labelling schemes already exist in Germany, Canada and Japan. Several other countries, including the Netherlands and France, are discussing setting up schemes.

Germany

The German 'Blue Angel' environmental labelling scheme is by far the longest-running, set up by the German Government in 1978. Around 3,000 products now carry the 'Blue Angel' logo, showing that they have met specific environmental criteria. These vary depending on the type of product, and are decided in consultation with representatives from consumer and environmental groups and industry. Once a product has been approved, the manufacturer pays an annual fee for the use of the logo. Examples of products covered include those which are reusable or recyclable (such as glass bottles) and those which use up fewer natural resources in the manufacturing process (such as recycled plastic and paper products). The scheme is voluntary and it hasn't prevented some manufacturers from continuing to devise their own environmental labels.

Canada

The Canadian environmental labelling scheme has been running for about a year. It is broadly similar to the German scheme, although more emphasis is placed on the environmental impact of a product throughout its life cycle. The first three product categories to carry the logo are re-refined motor oil, insulation material made from recycled paper, and a range of products made from recycled plastic. Other product types being considered include sanitary paper products made from recycled paper and a range of products made from recycled plastic.

Japan

Japan's labelling scheme is similar to the other two and has also been running for about a year. Products may be approved if they fall into one of a number of environmental categories. For example, one category denotes that the product causes minimal environmental damage when being used. Another denotes that the product causes minimal environmental damage when disposed of. Products which have received the logo include CFC-free sprays, and books and magazines printed on recycled paper. The logo appears on a product along with a brief explanation of why the product has been approved.

(© *Which?* Jan, 1990)

Figure 18.4

VOL 20 No 11 NOVEMBER 1990

SURVEY of Current Affairs

ENVIRONMENTAL PROTECTION ACT

The Environmental Protection Bill, which received Royal Assent on 1 November, makes a number of major changes to Britain's structure of environmental protection. These include:

- the introduction of a system of integrated pollution control;
- tougher regulations on waste disposal;
- a streamlined system for dealing with statutory nuisances;
- new powers and duties to deal with litter;
- controls on the use of genetically modified organisms;
- the reorganisation of the Nature Conservancy Council and the Countryside Commission; and
- increased penalties for polluting controlled waters.

Significant amendments have been made to the Act since January, when it received its second reading in the House of Commons. Among these are:

- reserve powers for the appropriate Secretary of State to set up regional Waste Regulation Authorities, if present initiatives for voluntary co-operation at regional level break down;
- a power for local authorities to collect abandoned shopping trolleys and charge their owners for their return;
- powers to obtain information about potentially harmful substances;
- public registers of land which may be contaminated;
- public registers about sea dumping and incineration;
- powers to ban the burning of crop residues; and
- the introduction of the Government's 'Action for Dogs' package, which includes measures for the collection and delivery of stray dogs, and enforcement of the existing collar and tag requirements.

The Minister for the Environment and Countryside, Mr David Trippier, welcomed the enactment and said that it was a landmark in the history of environmental legislation in Britain. The Act created a complete framework for pollution control into the next century, and would affect everyone, from major industrial corporations to individual citizens. Some of the measures, notably integrated pollution control, were as sophisticated as any in the world. 'This Act will further enhance our domestic environment and contribute significantly to the development of international environmental policy.'

Source: Department of the Environment new release, 1.11.90.

(Survey of Current Affairs, Nov. 1990)

INVESTIGATION OF BUSINESS TERMS

Consumerism. This is the means by which people can influence both the nature of output and production methods by deliberately altering their pattern of spending and hence consumption.

Statutory nuisances. This refers essentially to the 1936 Public Health Act which allows legal actions to be taken against those organizations or individuals who allow premises to become a health hazard or dispose of waste into rivers or the atmosphere.

SHORT-ANSWER QUESTIONS

1. How can a government subsidy to British Rail help to alleviate the 'greenhouse' effect?

2. Why will government schemes aimed at encouraging a more efficient use of energy by industrial and commercial concerns make a major contribution to tackling the 'greenhouse' effect?

3. How can the government use the taxation system to encourage manufacturers of electrical appliances and cars to pay more attention to energy consumption?

4. What business opportunities would exist for firms if the government took greater action to encourage energy conservation in the heating and lighting of homes?

5. Suggest how a business could exploit its use of recycled materials for its packaging and containers as part of its marketing.

6. Why is it likely that increased demand for organic food will lead to lower prices and the growth of this part of the food sector?

7. Should the awarding of an environmental stamp of approval be the responsibility of the government or an independent agency?

ANALYSING BUSINESS SITUATIONS

1. Are the present laws relating to consumer protection capable of dealing with claims concerning products and the environment?

2. Consider the implications for brewery and soft-drink manufacturers of a new law which introduced a minimum deposit on all glass and metal beverage containers.

3. Under the government's 'Integrated Pollution Control' system there will be inbuilt measures to ensure that standards are raised as technology improves. What loop-holes are the government attempting to close?

4. Is it fair that companies which produce toxic waste, for example, should be held responsible for any illegal dumping of such waste by another company contracted to dispose of it?

5. Examine the case for information on local levels of air pollution being given through regular local broadcasting rather than the public having to ask for such information.

6. Describe the possible effects upon the following types of businesses of the approach taken to environmental protection:

(a) a brewery;
(b) a scrap yard;
(c) a tannery;
(d) a demolition firm;
(e) a paint manufacturer;
(f) a pig farm;
(g) a road haulage firm;
(h) an arable farm.

ACTIVITIES

INVESTIGATION

(a) The class should be divided into five groups and each group should select one of the following categories of product:
  (i) paper goods;
  (ii) cars;
  (iii) cosmetics and personal toiletries;
  (iv) household cleaners;
  (v) food and drink.

(b) Each group should examine a range of items from its selected category and record information which relates to the environment, together with any 'official' looking environmental stamp.

(c) Analyse the information and the extent to which it makes:
  (i) excessive claims;
  (ii) multiple claims;
  (iii) claims which aren't explained;
  (iv) meaningless claims;
  (v) unrealistic claims.

(d) Having considered the actions taken by other countries to protect the environment, and the results of your investigations, outline a scheme for environmental labelling in the UK. Suggest appropriate penalties for firms when in breach of the regulations.

19

Government and small firms

Figure 19.1

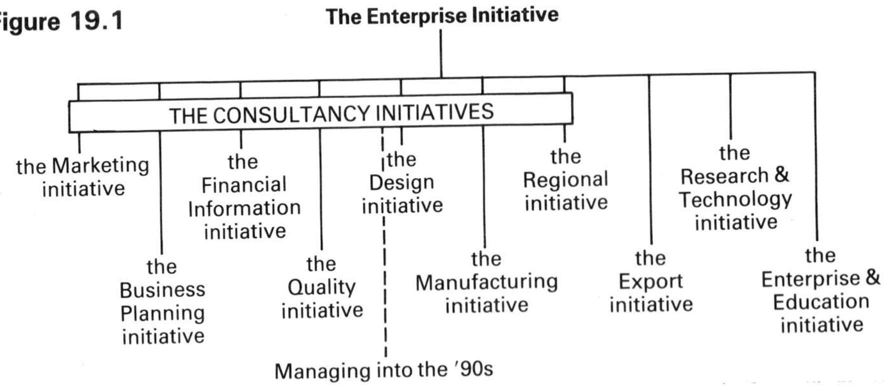

Figure 19.2

About the Enterprise Initiative

The Enterprise Initiative is DTI's comprehensive, self-help package of advice, guidance and practical help for British Business. It aims to provide the tools that business needs to increase its competitiveness and achieve its potential. It can help to develop your business in a number of ways, for example, by:

- putting you in touch with experts who can develop or provide key management skills, or giving you advice on best management practices,
- providing practical advice and assistance if you are exporting or planning to export,
- giving you access to collaborative research projects and providing information about technological developments as well as providing help to develop innovative ideas,
- helping you to forge links with local schools, universities and polytechnics,
- providing special assistance for firms in the Urban Programme Areas and the Assisted Areas.

There has never been a better time to think about building up your business. Read this brochure to find out what is available under the Enterprise Initiative. Then take it!

The Single European Market

Rapid progress towards completion of the Single Market by the end of 1992 is already being made and every firm should therefore be preparing now. The freer trading conditions of the Single Market will affect all firms in one way or another, whether their business is solely in the UK, elsewhere in the Community, or further afield. DTI provides a comprehensive range of information on the Single Market, including fact sheets on the Single Market programme, standards booklets, and action checklists, which is available through DTI's *1992 hotline* 01-200 1992. The Enterprise Initiative can help firms act on this information, to be ready for the Single Market challenge.

Business and the Environment

Protecting the environment is now a major issue both at home and abroad. Consumers are increasingly demanding goods which are environmentally friendly and pollution control standards are likely to get tighter. You will need to respond to these demands to remain competitive and the Enterprise Initiative can offer help on a wide variety of environmental issues. These are highlighted throughout this booklet and more detailed information on environmental pollution issues that affect business is available through DTI's *Environmental Enquiry Point* on 0800 585 794.

Figure 19.3

REGIONAL ENTERPRISE GRANTS

What assistance is available?

- grants for **investment** projects in most manufacturing and some service sectors. We will pay 15% of expenditure on fixed assets in the project, up to a maximum grant of £15,000. Eligible costs include plant and machinery (new or second-hand), buildings, purchase of land and site preparation, and vehicles used solely on site.
- grants for **innovation** projects which lead to the development and introduction of new or improved products and processes. We will pay 50% of eligible costs, up to a maximum grant of £25,000. All costs up to the point of commercial production may be assisted, including capital costs directly associated with the project. Work can range from feasibility studies, through the development of technical specifications, to the design and manufacture of prototypes. It can be subcontracted where appropriate.
  There is no limit on the size of projects which can be considered.

Am I eligible?

You are eligible if
- you are an individual, partnership, company or part of a group with fewer than 25 employees (full-time equivalent) world-wide. A group of companies is one where the company and any other company are associated or related or have in common a substantial shareholder or group of shareholders, and
- your project will take place in a **Development Area** (see the map of Assisted Areas in this leaflet) or **South Yorkshire***.

The European Community does not allow, or limits, the payment of grant to projects in certain sectors. EC restrictions currently apply to man-made fibre and yarn, isoglucose, shipbuilding and ship repair, iron and steel, fisheries, milk and milk substitutes.

Service sector projects which serve only a local market (like retailing), would not normally qualify for an investment grant. They may qualify for an innovation grant. Banks and insurance companies are not eligible.

What criteria will the Department apply?

We need to be satisfied that your business and your project are viable. The best way for us to assess that is for you to send us a **business statement** or **plan** which
- gives a brief description of your business and the roles of key personnel
- explains how you see your business developing over the next 2 or 3 years. What are the market opportunities?
- describes how the project fits in to your plans. What effect do you expect it to have on current sales, profit, employment levels?
- gives details of how the project and your business will be financed.

Your plan does not need to be in any special format. If you need help in preparing a business plan, the regionally based Small Firms Service run by the Department of Employment, or the Rural Development Commission, or your local enterprise agency, may be able to help.

For **innovation** projects we will be looking for a degree of novelty and technical risk. For projects aimed at product development there needs to be an improvement or advance on your business' product range. Process development projects should be able to demonstrate a likely significant increase in efficiency.

How to apply

Complete the enclosed application form – **attach your business plan and latest accounts** – and send it to your nearest local office. A full list of addresses is given in this leaflet.

The payment of grant will be subject to certain terms and conditions which will be detailed in the letter we send you offering a grant.

Important

Please remember – it is very difficult to establish that you need our support if you have already started work on the project. **You are strongly advised not to start your project until you have applied for assistance and received an offer.**

How many times can I apply?

You can receive only one investment and one innovation grant. You may receive both but not for the same project costs.

Regional selective assistance

An alternative form of support for investment projects undertaken by firms in Development and Intermediate Areas is available through Regional Selective Assistance.

The project must be commercially viable, create or safeguard employment, demonstrate a need for assistance, and offer a distinct regional and national benefit. The amount of grant will be negotiated as the minimum necessary to ensure the project goes ahead. Simplified procedures apply to applications for grants of £25,000 or less.

If you are interested in this form of support, contact your nearest Regional Office, Scottish Office or Welsh Office for a copy of the Guide to Regional Selective Assistance.

Important – you cannot receive a Regional Enterprise Grant and Regional Selective Assistance for the same project.

Publicity

Accepted offers may be publicised by means of press releases giving brief descriptive details of the project and the grant amount.

* Regional Enterprise Grants are available in the Barnsley, Doncaster and Sheffield Travel-to-Work Areas as part of the European Regional Development Fund's Community Programme for steel areas (RESIDER). Other areas may become eligible under RESIDER or the parallel programme for shipbuilding areas (RENAVAL) in the future.

Figure 19.4

Intermediate Areas

Development Areas

Urban Programme Areas
Outside Assisted Areas

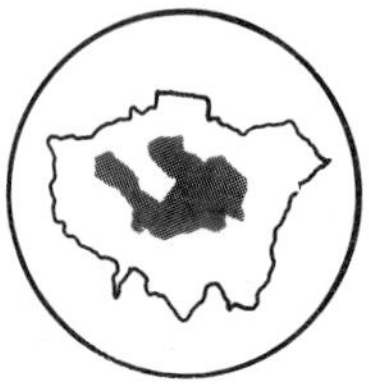

Urban Programme Areas in London

Contact Points
1 Scotland
2 DTI North East
3 DTI Yorkshire and Humberside
4 DTI North West *(Manchester)*
5 DTI North East *(Liverpool)*
6 DTI East Midlands
7 DTI West Midlands
8 DTI East
9 DTI South East *(London)*
10 DTI South East *(Reading)*
11 DTI South East *(Reigate)*
12 DTI South West
13 Wales

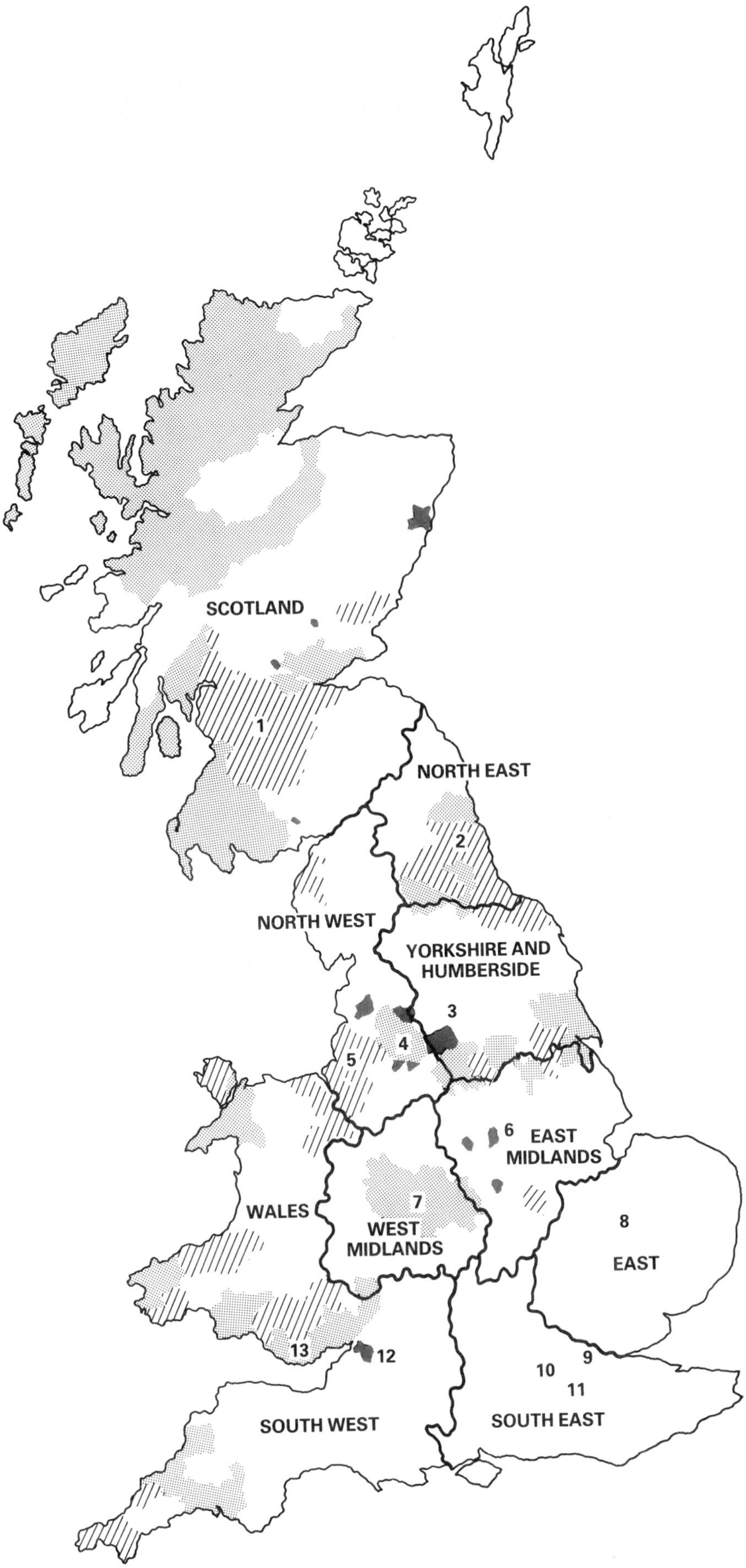

The Assisted Areas are the Development Areas and Intermediate Areas as defined by DTI at 29.11.84

All material in this Unit reproduced with kind permission from the Department of Trade and Industry

DTI. The government's Department of Trade and Industry which encourages enterprise through promoting trade both at home and abroad. The DTI aids the development of industry in general, and the small-firms sector and the regions in particular. As such it provides grants, advice and consultancy services and acts as the channel through which European Community support is provided.

Feasibility study. An investigation carried out to assess whether a proposed commercial or industrial project is likely to be worthwhile.

Full-time equivalent. This is used in order to calculate the size of the workforce, make comparisons, undertake manpower planning and to carry out costings. This involves combining the hours of part-time workers, and then dividing them by the normal full-time working-day to produce the equivalent in terms of full-time workers.

SHORT-ANSWER QUESTIONS

1. Why does the United Kingdom need an organization such as the DTI?
2. Explain what the DTI means by 'encouraging enterprise'.
3. Outline the advantages to firms of being involved in (a) collaborative research projects, and (b) increased links with local schools, colleges and universities.
4. Explain why the DTI provides special assistance in the urban areas.
5. Justify the DTI's concern in promoting goods which are environmentally friendly.
6. Suggest why the government is more generous towards innovative projects rather than to straightforward investment.
7. Explain why the government is prepared to help with the costs of a feasibility study and other stages right up to the manufacture of a prototype, but refuses to help with the commercial production and subsequent running costs of the venture.
8. What is the link between measuring employees as full-time equivalents and the criteria for securing DTI support?
9. Explain why the European Community Regional Enterprise Grants cover whole areas around such places as Barnsley, Doncaster and Sheffield.
10. Suggest why the government's Regional Selective Assistance has the potential for being more generous.

The Budget

Figure 20.1

THE BUDGET

in brief

Published by
The Treasury
10 March 1992

The Budget reaffirms the Government's commitment to a low tax, low inflation economy. Over the last year, inflation has fallen sharply and interest rates have been reduced. Despite the world economic slowdown, economic growth is expected to resume in 1992. The central plank of the Government's economic policy is membership of the ERM, underpinned by product management of the public finances.

The measures announced in the Budget will benefit all tax payers by cutting the starting rate of income tax, and will provide extra help for poorer pensioners. They will give a boost to businesses generally and to the car industry in particular. The Government is also proposing a fundamental reform of the Budget process.

Personal taxes

The Chancellor proposes to cut the rate of income tax to 20 per cent on the first £2,000 of taxable income. This is a significant step towards the Government's target of a basic rate of 20 per cent. It will reduce the starting rate of income tax and allow those on lower incomes to keep more out of every extra £1 of income. With other income tax changes, most taxpayers will be about £2.64 a week better off.

The Chancellor also proposes to:

- increase the income tax personal allowance and age-related allowances in line with inflation;
- allow couples to choose, by agreement, to transfer the married couple's allowance from husband to wife or to share it equally. Or the wife will be able to claim half the allowance at her own request;
- make no change to the basic rate limit or the married couple's allowance for those under 65;
- allow single gifts to charities of £400 or more (down from £600) to qualify for tax relief under the Gift Aid scheme;
- allow savings in qualifying unit and investment trusts through PEPs up to the full £6,000 limit, instead of £3,000 as now;
- raise the threshold for inheritance tax by more than inflation, to £150,000;
- raise the annual exempt amount for capital gains tax to £5,800 in line with inflation.

Extra help for poorer pensioners

The Chancellor announced that there would be extra help too for poorer pensioners. From October, single pensioners on income support will get an extra £2 a week, and married couples an extra £3 a week.

Reform of the Budget

Tax and expenditure decisions will be brought together and announced at the same time in a Budget which will take place in December each year. This will mean better decision taking and clearer presentation. It will bring practice in the UK into line with that in most other developed countries.

The Chancellor has issued a White Paper with a view to making the switch in December 1993; the last Budget on the present timetable will therefore be in spring 1993.

Other main features

- **Business rates** to be cut by £480 million in 1992–3.
- A range of other **measures to help business**, including cuts in VAT penalties and exemption of most business assets from inheritance tax.
- A package to reduce discrimination in the tax system against cars, including the halving of **car tax** to 5 per cent and relaxation of the restriction on **capital allowances** for business cars.
- **Excise duties** on alcohol, diesel and unleaded petrol increased in line with prices; duty on leaded petrol raised by 7½ per cent and the duty on cigarettes raised by about 10 per cent (pipe tobacco indexed). Vehicle excise duty on cars raised by £10 to £110.

(Treasury (HMSO), 10 March 1992)

Figure 20.1 (cont.)

Table 1
Income tax allowance

£	1991-92	1992-93
Personal	3,295	3,445
Married couple's, additional personal and widow's bereavement	1,720	1,720
Lower rate limit	—	2,000
Basic rate limit[1]	23,700	23,700
Aged 65-74:		
personal	4,020	4,200
married couple's	2,335	2,465
Aged 75 and over:		
personal	4,180	4,370
married couple's	2,395	2,505
Age-related income limit	13,500	14,200

1 Basic rate limit in 1992-93 is the first £23,000 of taxable income i.e. including £2,000 subject to lower rate.

Table 2
PSBR projections and economic assumptions over the medium term[1]

	1991-2	1992-3	1993-4	1994-5	1995-6	1996-7
PSBR (per cent of GDP)	2¼	4½	4¾	3½	2½	¾
Money GDP growth[2]	5	6½	6¾	6¾	6	5¼
Real GDP growth[2]:						
- Non-North Sea	−2¼	1¾	3	3½	3½	3½
- Total	−2	2	3¼	3¾	3¾	3¼
Inflation[2]						
GDP deflator	7	4½	3½	3	2½	2

1 Forecasts for 1992-93 and illustrative projections thereafter.
2 Percentage changes on previous financial year.

Economic background

Inflation has fallen sharply over the last year. Retail price inflation in January was 4 per cent, less than half its rate at the beginning of 1991 and below the average for EC countries. Over the same period earnings growth has slowed from 9½ per cent to 7¼ per cent, its lowest rate since 1967. Interest rates have been reduced by 4½ percentage points since ERM entry was announced. [See Figure 20.2 on page 54]

Activity levelled out in the second half of 1991. But signs of recovery last summer and early autumn were not sustained. This was part of a pattern of weakening activity in most of the major countries; domestic demand remained weak as individuals and companies increased their saving.

With inflation and interest rates substantially lower, and consumer and business confidence stronger than a year ago, activity is expected to recover in 1992. GDP is forecast to rise by 2 per cent in the year to the second half of 1992, so that for the year as a whole it is up by 1 per cent on 1991.

Underlying inflation is expected to fall steadily through 1992. RPI inflation may pick up a little in the next few months as special factors drop out. But it is forecast to fall to 3¾ per cent by the fourth quarter, and to 3¼ per cent by mid-1993. Producer output price inflation (excluding food, drink and tobacco) is forecast to come down to 1½ per cent by mid-1993. The current account deficit is forecast to rise from £4½ billion in 1991 to £6½ billion in 1992, as domestic demand recovers.

Economic strategy

The Medium Term Financial Strategy (MTFS) sets out the Government's approach to monetary and fiscal policy. The central objective of the MTFS is the defeat of inflation. Permanently low inflation is essential for a healthy economy and the success of other policies designed to improve the flexibility and efficiency of markets.

The Government's commitment to the Exchange Rate Mechanism (ERM) of the European Monetary System provides the framework for monetary policy, and is the main discipline underpinning macroeconomic policy in the medium term. It means that UK inflation will move progressively into line with the best inflation performance in other ERM countries. All members of the ERM are firmly committed to the objective of price stability, and the Government will set monetary and fiscal policy to achieve this outcome. [See Figure 20.3 on page 54]

The Government is retaining the present target range 0 to 4 per cent for narrow money (M0), and will continue to monitor broad money and credit carefully. But in setting interest rates it will continue to give overriding priority to maintaining sterling within its ERM bands. In due course the Government will move to the narrow bands of the ERM, at the central rate of 2.95 Deutschemarks.

Fiscal policy is set in a medium term context. The Government's objective is to balance the budget over the medium term, while permitting the "automatic stabilisers" to operate. This approach is designed to ensure that a firm fiscal stance supports monetary policy in achieving low inflation, while the PSBR varies with the cyclical position of the economy.

The Budget sets a PSBR of £28 billion for 1992–93. This reflects the lagged impact of the recession on both expenditure and revenue. The budget is projected to return steadily towards balance in the medium term as activity recovers.

The Budget and business

The Chancellor announced a number of measures to help business. These come on top of the cut to 33 per cent in the main rate of corporation tax announced in the last Budget. With other changes in corporation tax introduced last year, this is already due to boost companies' cash flow in 1992–93 by some £1 billion.

This year the Chancellor announced a package worth £480 million in 1992–93 and £590 million in 1993–94 to non-domestic ratepayers:

- no business will face an increase in its rates bill for 1992–93 above the rate of inflation;
- businesses moving to lower bills under the new rates system in England and Wales will receive their gains in full in 1993–94 and will get larger reductions in their bills in 1992–93;
- businesses moving premises will inherit any transitional relief from the previous owners;
- businesses in Scotland and Northern Ireland will also benefit under their different rates systems.

The Chancellor also announced measures to:

- exempt most business assets from inheritance tax so that most family businesses can be passed on without a tax charge;
- reduce VAT penalties;
- require Government contractors to pay their bills to suppliers promptly;
- allow the largest businesses to pay VAT monthly on account instead of submitting monthly returns;
- improve the tax treatment of film expenditure;
- make it easier to use the Business Expansion Scheme (BES) for mortgage rescue schemes. The BES will finish at the end of 1993 (when relief for assured tenancy schemes was already due to expire).

20

Figure 20.1 (cont.)

Cars

The Chancellor also announced a package to reduce discrimination in the tax system against cars.

He proposes to:

- Halve the rate of car tax to 5 per cent;
- lift restrictions on businesses claiming capital allowances on cars costing £12,000 or less;
- allow driving schools, taxi and self-drive hire firms to recover VAT when they buy cars;
- raise income tax car and petrol scale charges in line with inflation, and consult on how to move to car scales based on the price of the car, not its engine size;
- recognise the lower cost of diesel by introducing lower fuel scale charges for diesel cars;
- stop charging VAT when firms offer employees a choice between a car or extra salary.

Excise duties

Increases in most excise duties take effect from 6pm on Budget day. The Chancellor proposes to:

- raise duties on alcohol in line with inflation. This will mean about 1p on the price of a typical pint of beer, about 5p on a bottle of wine, and about 28p on a bottle of scotch whisky;
- raise duty on unleaded petrol and diesel by 4½ per cent, in line with inflation. This will mean 1.2p on a litre of unleaded petrol;
- raise duty on leaded petrol by 7½ per cent. This will mean 2.3p on a litre of leaded petrol and will raise the difference between taxes on leaded and unleaded petrol from 4p to 5.1p a litre;
- raise duty on cigarettes and other tobacco by about 10 per cent, with the exception of pipe tobacco which will rise in line with inflation. This will mean 13p on the price of 20 cigarettes, and 8p on 50g of pipe tobacco;
- raise vehicle excise duty on cars by £10 to £110, but freeze duty on lorries.

The Chancellor also promises to cut the rate of betting duty to 7¾ per cent, from 1 April. Most of the benefit will go to horseracing through a higher levy on betting. Extra help for greyhound racing will also be explored.

Figure 20.2
Interest rates

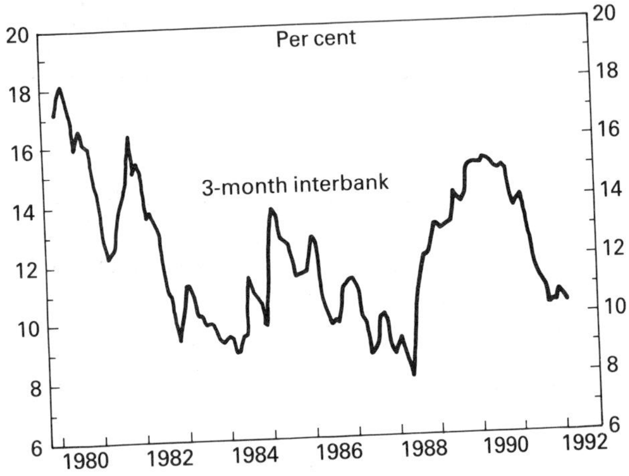

Figure 20.3
Public sector borrowing requirement[1]

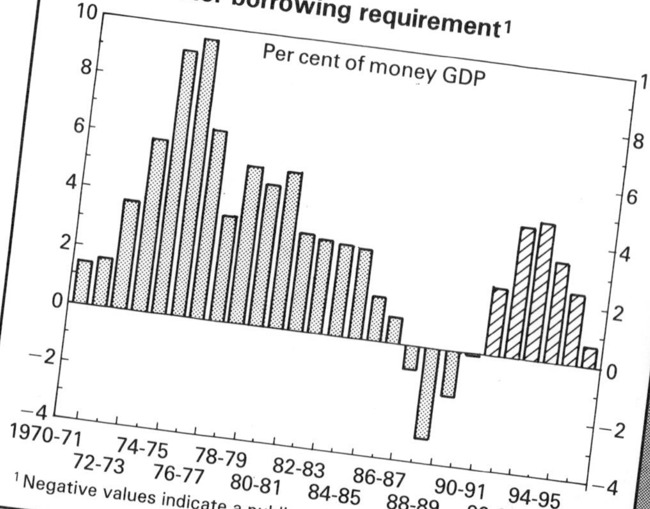

[1] Negative values indicate a public sector debt repayment

Money GDP refers to Gross Domestic Product valued at current prices and is widely regarded as a good guide to underlying inflationary pressures.

MO covers cash in circulation with the public and the banks plus commercial banks' working balances at the Bank of England.

Exchange Rate Mechanism (ERM) refers to that part of the European Monetary System which EC members are free to join. Under this mechanism the member countries are expected to maintain their exchange rates against all other countries within permitted margins of fluctuation. This may require member states to take such policy actions as the raising or lowering of interest rates, or intervening in the foreign exchange markets. The advantage of the ERM is that it should result in greater exchange rate stability, which makes trade and capital movements easier and cheaper.

Public Sector Borrowing Requirement (PSBR) refers to the excess of public sector spending over public sector revenue. It can be financed either by selling liquid assets to the banking private sector, or by borrowing. The former will cause an increase in money GDP, whereas the latter may drive interest rates upwards.

SHORT-ANSWER QUESTIONS

1. How might the Budget procedure be reformed? What is the argument in favour of such action?
2. How might the inflation of the late 1980s have been avoided?
3. Suggest why MO is considered to be the most reliable monetary indicator.
4. Examine the ways in which the 1992 Budget was of particular benefit to small businesses.
5. Explain how the ERM links the UK inflation rate to that of other countries within Europe.
6. How do you feel that the Friends of the Earth might have reacted to the Budget?
7. Outline the ways in which the Budget reflects the changing role of women within both society in general and the workforce in particular.
8. How does the medium-term financial strategy control the demand for money in both the private and public sectors?

ANALYSING BUSINESS SITUATIONS

1. What factors would have contributed to the fall of inflation between January 1991 and January 1992?
2. Examine the case for the government running a balanced budget.
3. Identify two ways in which inflation may be said to affect a firm adversely and two ways in which it might be said to benefit a firm.

   Suggest two policy measures the government could use to control inflation which would affect the demand for a firm's products.
4. Assume that you are employed as a business analyst working for a Japanese multinational car company operating in the UK. It is your job to analyse the effects of the 1992 Budget.

   Make a list outlining how the following might be affected:

   (a) the overall economic and financial environment in which the company operates;
   (b) the company's customers and clients;
   (c) the various operations of the company and its future prospects.
5. Explain how membership of the ERM might be said to have acted as a restraint on the government's monetary policy.

ACTIVITIES

ESSAYS

1. **(a)** Explain how a change in interest rates alters opportunity costs for a firm.

   (b) Identify areas of organizational activity that might be particularly affected by such a change. (Cambridge, June 1989)
2. Analyse the strategies available to a firm to enable it to survive a period of recession in its home markets. (AEB, Nov. 1987)
3. Examine how an enterprise might alter its plans if a prolonged period of heavy unemployment is predicted. (AEB, June 1988)

International competitiveness

Figure 21.1 THE UK'S VISIBLE TRADE

When the UK economy suffers from a persistent and growing deficit on its trade with the rest of the world then this is evidence that the UK producers in general are finding it increasingly difficult to compete with overseas producers. Such a loss of international competitiveness and the resulting trade deficit can be caused by several factors:

- If UK companies give their employees pay increases in excess of improvements in productivity this will mean a rise in unit labour costs and in order to protect their profit margins they will be obliged to increase their prices. Higher prices will not only make UK producers less competitive in export markets but also weaken their position when facing competition from imports.
- International competitiveness can also be damaged by insufficient attention being paid to non-price factors such as quality, design and style, performance, delivery and after-sales services.
- Firms involved in high-technology capital goods may not have devoted sufficient resources to the kinds of research-and-development projects that lead to new and improved products and processes.
- A lack of investment in additional and more efficient productive capacity may leave some producers in a situation where they are unable to cope with a sudden upturn in the demand for their products on the home market. They may therefore lose market share to overseas producers who can offer more competitive delivery dates.
- A more buoyant home demand may also cause those UK firms with a shortage of capacity to switch more of their resources to satisfying the home market at the expense of a much reduced export effort.
- Skills shortages may also be a major factor in preventing UK producers from expanding output to meet a higher demand. Such skills shortages will also lead to higher pay settlements and hence unit costs as employers seek to both retain and attract certain types of labour.

	Exports	Imports	£M Visible balance
1980	47,147	45,792	+ 1,355
1981	50,668	47,418	+ 3,250
1982	55,331	53,421	+ 1,910
1983	60,700	62,237	− 1,537
1984	70,265	75,601	− 5,336
1985	77,991	81,336	− 3,345
1986	72,656	82,141	− 9,485
1987	79,446	90,669	−11,223
1988	80,776	101,854	−21,078
1989	92,792	116,632	−23,840

Figure 21.2

UK exports and imports[a] (seasonally adjusted)

	Exports							Imports							
	Total	Non-manufactures		Manufactures				Total	Non-manufactures			Manufactures			
		Total	Fuels	Total	Semis (b)	Finished (b)	UK share of world exports		Food, Beverages, tobacco	Basic materials	Fuels	Total	Semis	Finished	UK imports as % of final expenditure
1980	83.7	58	58	91	93	89	105	78.9	87	98	115	71	82	65	10.8
1981	82.6	76	70	85	85	86	96	75.8	90	92	94	70	75	67	10.1
1982	85.3	81	78	87	86	87	102	80.3	94	91	86	77	80	75	10.7
1983	87.2	88	86	87	91	84	99	87.2	94	102	77	87	90	85	11.7
1984	94.5	95	93	94	97	93	98	96.5	98	100	100	95	97	95	12.7
1985	100.0	100	100	100	100	100	100	100.0	100	100	100	100	100	100	12.8
1986	104.0	105	104	104	106	102	102	107.2	109	107	107	107	108	106	12.9
1987	109.8	104	101	112	113	112	105	114.8	109	117	105	118	118	118	13.3
1988	113.0	98	94	120	122	120	103	131.2	115	118	108	140	135	142	14.0
1989	117.8	88	75	132	126	136	104	140.2	118	117	114	151	142	157	14.5

Note: Volume index numbers, 1985 = 100.

(NIESR, Aug. 1990)

(a) On overseas trade statistics basis

(b) Less erratic items (i.e. ships, North Sea oil production installations, aircraft, precious stones and silver).

Figure 21.3

Consumers' expenditure and credit (seasonally adjusted)

	Consumers' expenditure		£ million, current prices				Total retail sales
	Durable goods	Non-durable goods	Consumer credit (a)	Bank lending		Building societies	Volume
	£ million, 1985 prices		Total	(b) Companies	(c) Personal	Mortgages	1985 = 100
1980	15,417	179,643	1,661	+ 5,937	+ 2,965	9,614	86
1981	15,707	179,466	2,473	+ 3,288	+ 3,990	11,991	86
1982	16,504	181,476	2,634	+ 1,848	+ 4,989	15,339	88
1983	19,452	187,654	3,287	+ 2,379	+ 4,893	19,263	92
1984	19,258	191,214	3,097	+ 5,719	+ 4,174	24,034	96
1985	20,251	197,690	3,820	+ 6,913	+ 6,655	26,491	100
1986	22,164	209,506	4,324	+ 8,380	+ 5,174	36,937	105
1987	24,541	219,483	5,947	+14,963	+ 8,654	35,529	112
1988	27,699	233,881	6,195	+30,486	+12,932	49,605	119
1989	29,330	242,377	5,878	+35,278	+13,597	45,160	122

(a) Amount outstanding at end of period.
(b) Industrial and commercial companies only.
(c) Excluding loans for house purchase.

(NIESR, Aug. 1990)

Figure 21.4

Consumer prices 1979–89

Year	US	Japan	France	Germany	UK	OECD total
79	88.1	92.6	87.5	94.8	84.8	88.6
80	100.0	99.8	100.7	100.0	100.0	100.0
81	110.3	104.7	113.8	106.3	111.9	110.5
82	117.1	107.6	126.7	111.9	121.5	119.1
83	120.8	109.7	138.7	115.6	127.1	125.3
84	126.0	112.1	148.9	118.4	133.5	131.7
85	130.5	114.4	157.9	121.0	141.6	137.7
86	132.9	115.1	161.2	120.8	146.4	141.2
87	137.9	115.2	166.7	121.2	152.5	145.8
88	143.6	116.0	171.4	122.7	159.9	151.5
89	150.5	118.7	176.8	126.1	172.4	164.1

Note: Index numbers, 1980 = 100, seasonally adjusted. (NIESR, Aug. 1990)

Figure 21.5

An increasing deficit on the UK's international trade will lead to developments in foreign exchange markets which put a downward pressure upon the exchange rate for the pound. Increasing quantities of pounds will be sold by people in the UK in order to buy the foreign currencies needed to pay for imports. At the same time the weaker export performance will mean a relatively low demand for pounds from people overseas exchanging their own currencies for the pounds needed to pay for UK exports. The supply of pounds onto foreign exchange markets will therefore exceed the demand for pounds. In the absence of any government intervention to support the price of the pound, i.e. the exchange rate, it will start to fall in value against the currencies of the other major manufacturing economies. The fall in the exchange rate may help to protect the competitive position of those UK producers who have raised their prices to cover increased costs. This is because the lower exchange rate will make UK exports cheaper to foreigners in terms of their own currencies while also raising the prices of competing imports on the UK market in terms of sterling.

Exchange rate for sterling – annual average

Year	US dollars	D-Marks	Effective exchange rate
80	2.32	4.25	100
81	2.02	4.55	98.9
82	1.75	4.24	90.2
83	1.51	3.87	86.7
84	1.34	3.79	81.9
85	1.30	3.78	81.5
86	1.48	3.18	75.8
87	1.64	2.94	75.6
88	1.78	3.12	68.1
89	1.64	3.08	59.0
90	1.79	2.87	57.5

Note: Index numbers 1980 = 100

Source: NIESR

(*Bank of England Quarterly Review* March 1983 and November 1990)

Figure 21.6a

If the UK government rules out a devaluation then it can respond to a downward pressure upon the exchange rate by raising interest rates in the UK. This will stimulate the demand for pounds from people overseas who will sell their own currencies in order to place their funds on deposit in the UK financial system. The excess supply of pounds on foreign exchange markets will therefore be mopped up by overseas investors and this will help to support the value of the pound.

Figure 21.6b

Why the ERM means British pay must slow

The Government's decision to link the pound to the German mark means that British interest rates now depend on sentiment in the foreign exchanges, and they can only fall in one of two sets of circumstances.

The first is where German interest rates fall. German rates are an effective floor to the ERM for a simple reason: if average European savers were given the choice of 9 per cent German interest rates or 9 per cent British interest rates, they would choose to hold their money in German marks. All the post-war track record suggests that German inflation will be lower than British inflation, so that the 9 per cent will be worth more in real terms.

Other ERM countries therefore have to keep their interest rates higher than German rates to compensate savers for their higher inflation, and the expected eventual fall in their currencies against the mark.

The second set of circumstances in which British interest rates can fall is if British inflation falls and the markets perceive that it will stay down. This in turn gives the Government a strong incentive to keep inflation down. The ERM is not a counter-inflationary device for nothing.

One of the ways the ERM exerts its anti-inflationary discipline is by linking British and German prices. Imagine what would happen if British inflation continued at a much higher rate than German inflation, and the pound were not devalued against the mark. German goods would hardly change in price, while British goods would become more expensive. Britain plc would gradually price itself out of markets.

What if British firms tried to compete by holding their prices down? British inflation would then fall. But if British firms' costs – notably wages, which account for more than half of all costs – were to go on rising at the old rate, their profits would be severely squeezed.

They would embark on another round of cost-cutting, which would involve lay-offs and redundancies. The rise in unemployment would eventually scare workers into accepting lower pay rises, and would thus bring the rise in business costs in line with the rise in their prices.

(Extracts from *Independent on Sunday*, 6 Jan. 1991)

Figure 21.7

Lamont fights pressure for base rate cut

THE Government is coming under strong pressure to lower interest rates in the face of fears that the UK recession is deepening and that the pound may have entered the European Monetary System's Exchange rate mechanism at too high a level.

With the preservation of exchange rate parity the most important consideration in monetary policy under the ERM's rules, Lamont has to face the fact that sterling is the weakest currency in the ERM band. It fell again on Friday to close at DM2.91 (against DM2.9225 the night before, and an official central rate of DM2.95).

There is growing concern in the City and in industry that the Government has underestimated the power of the recessionary forces in the economy. Last week the chairman of ICI, Sir Denys Henderson, told business economists in London that 'there is little likelihood of a pick-up until the second half of 1991 at the earliest'.

One of the factors behind Henderson's pessimism is ICI's belief that the Government has put the pound into the ERM at too high a level.

ICI economists appear to agree with Mrs Thatcher's former economic adviser, Sir Alan Walters, that a central rate of closer to DM2.60 would have been more appropriate. Sir Alan has argued that Britain faces a deeper recession than the rest of the world precisely because of its exchange rate policy.

ICI's chief economist, Richard Freeman, states in a paper that 'there is no doubt sterling is over-valued against the DM' and quotes with approval an analysis by John Williamson, of the Institute of International Economics in Washington, one of the leading authorities on exchange rates, that the overvaluation is 'about 10 per cent'.

(Extracts from *Observer*, 2 Dec. 1990)

Figure 21.8

Britain's pay rise problem.....

Percentage increase in wages per head over year

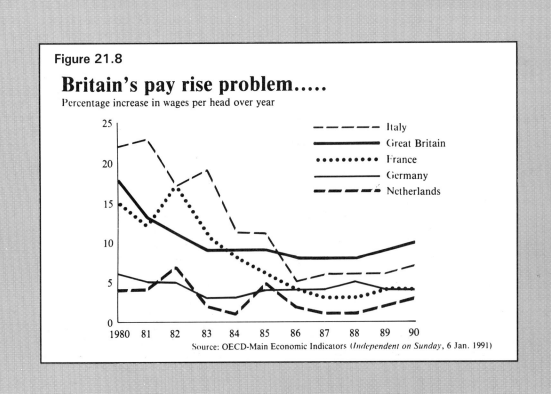

Source: OECD-Main Economic Indicators (*Independent on Sunday*, 6 Jan. 1991)

SHORT-ANSWER QUESTIONS

1. What are the problems facing a UK producer in seeking to regain its market share lost to imports?
2. What developments can lead to a large and sudden increase in the level of consumer expenditure?
3. Why can a more buoyant demand for cars lead to an increase in the import of a wide range of manufactures?
4. A UK exporter has labour costs of £300,000 for every 10,000 units of output. What will be the effect upon unit labour costs if productivity rises by 6 per cent while at the same time the employees negotiate a pay increase of 14 per cent?
5. Give examples of high-technology products where expenditure on research and development will be a major factor in determining international competitiveness.
6. Distinguish between semi-manufactures and finished manufactures. Why is the growth of the latter of particular concern to the government?
7. Why will a fall in the value of the pound be of little benefit to those producers whose sales are currently inhibited by a lack of investment in productive capacity?
8. What do you understand by the UK being in recession?
9. 'During the 1980s, workers in Germany received percentage pay increases which were lower than those in the UK. German workers, however, still enjoyed a much higher purchasing power than their counterparts in the UK.' Explain this statement.
10. 'UK membership of the European exchange rate mechanism will exert a greater discipline over pay settlements and oblige UK producers to avoid price increases which are greater than those in Germany. A decision to allow a fall in the exchange rate would only open the way for a further round of excessive pay and price increases.' Explain and evaluate this statement.
11. Explain why a fall in the rate of inflation in the UK relative to that in Germany and a subsequent improvement in the trade balance would allow the government to cut interest rates in the UK.
12. Why did some economists believe that the value of the pound should have been allowed to fall to a lower and more realistic level before joining the European exchange rate mechanism?

ANALYSING BUSINESS SITUATIONS

1. During a period of rising demand, why may some firms be obliged to grant large pay increases to retain and attract labour, despite being in areas where there are relatively high levels of unemployment?
2. With the use of examples, describe how various non-price factors can be of particular importance in determining the competitive position of UK producers in relation to the following kinds of imports:

(a) clothing and footwear;
(b) consumer durables;
(c) motor vehicle parts and components;
(d) plant, machinery and equipment.

3. Explain why developments in technology mean that the UK's imports of basic (raw) materials grow less rapidly than imports of manufacturers.
4. Assume that a UK exporter with customers in Germany was selling a product at £1,500, but during the course of the following year is obliged to raise this price by 8 per cent to cover increased costs. At the same time, the exchange rate for the pound falls from DM 3.00 to DM 2.60. Calculate the combined effect of these developments upon the price of the product to customers in Germany.
5. A US manufacturer of computers is selling a particular item of equipment at $4,000. What is the effect upon the price of this product in the UK market if the value of the pound falls from $2.00 to $1.75?
6. A UK producer has unit costs of £40 and 25 per cent of these costs are accounted for by imported parts and components from Japan while a further 15 per cent of costs are associated with imported raw materials priced in US dollars. The exchange rate for the pound against the Japanese yen is currently Y240 and against the US dollar it is $2. What would be the effect upon this producer's unit costs if the pound depreciates by 10 per cent against the yen and 15 per cent against the US dollar?
7. Assume that a rise in UK rate of interest attracts large inflows of capital from abroad and that the resulting demand for pounds actually leads to a rise in the value of the pound against other major currencies. With the use of a numerical example, explain how this will affect the following:

(a) a UK manufacturer which imports parts and components;
(b) the price of a UK product on a foreign market;
(c) a UK producer facing competition from an imported product.

8. Describe the problems which would face UK producers if the exchange rate for the pound was susceptible to unpredictable and significant fluctuations on foreign exchange markets.
9. Despite a marked fall in the value of the pound during the 1980s, the UK continued to suffer from a growing trade deficit. Give possible reasons why many UK manufacturers still had greater difficulty in meeting intense competition from overseas producers.

ACTIVITIES

INVESTIGATION

1. Calculate the annual percentage changes in the 1980s in the UK's exports and imports of semi-manufactures and finished manufactures. Plot these changes on graph paper, ensuring that the vertical scale is such that movements are clearly illustrated. Discuss these changes in relation to the following:

(a) consumer expenditure;
(b) consumer credit, bank lending and mortgage advances;
(c) the rate of inflation in the UK relative to that in other economies.

2. Over a period of time, collect articles and data from the quality newspapers which deal with the following:

(a) the rate of inflation in the UK compared with other major manufacturing economies;
(b) level of earnings and pay settlements;
(c) improvements in productivity;
(e) exports and imports.

Use this information to outline those developments which are likely to influence the future competitive position of UK firms in relation to overseas producers.

ESSAYS

(a) What do you understand by the phrases 'market share', 'import penetration' and 'cross elasticity of demand'.
(b) How might a UK-based firm attempt to counteract the problems of increasing foreign competition? If you wish, you may choose to confine your answer to a specific industry (University of Cambridge, June, 1988)

22

The effects of deflation

Figure 22.1

Total demand expands faster than the rate at which total output can be increased

Imports rise to satisfy demand

Inflation is higher than the average for other manufacturing economies.

An increasing deficit on the balance of trade

The Government deflates total demand:-
- Higher interest rates
- Credit controls
- Higher taxation
- Cuts in Government spending

Imports start to fall because:-
- Lower household demand will reduce spending on imported consumer goods
- The fall in the level of domestic output will reduce imports of energy, raw materials, parts, etc.
- The fall in domestic demand will allow UK firms to offer improved delivery dates compared with imports
- Inflation falls below that in other countries and imports become less attractive relative to home produced goods and services.

Exports start to rise because:-
- Home producers are forced to seek export markets to maintain sales
- The fall in domestic demand will allow home producers to offer improved delivery dates to overseas customers
- Inflation falls and exports become more competitive in overseas markets.

An improvement in the UK's trade balance.

Figure 22.2

Business failures reach record high

BUSINESS failures in England and Wales reached a record high in 1990. More than 24,000 enterprises collapsed during the year, topping the previous high of 21,682 in 1984 during the last recession, said business information group Dun & Bradstreet.

Its surveys date back to 1980 but marketing manager Philip Mellor said the 1990 figure represented an all-time high.

'It is very disturbing that the level of business failures is now running annually nearly twice as high as it was 10 years ago.

All the signs are that for the foreseeable future the situation will get worse rather than improve,' he said.

Total business collapses in England and Wales rose a record 34.6 per cent to 24,442 in 1990. Company liquidations increased 33.5 per cent to 13,611 and bankruptcies among individuals, firms and partnerships were up 36 per cent at 10,831.

Southern England suffered more than northern areas and the South-west had the highest increase, with the number of failures up 70 per cent to more than 3,000, compared with the previous year.

Failures in eastern regions rose by 50 per cent while the North-east and North-west recorded increases of about 20 per cent.

Mr Mellor said many firms were not applying basic procedures to safeguard their cash flow in the tough economic climate. Small businesses were particularly vulnerable as a result of high interest rates and falling consumer demand.

A Labour Party survey claimed the small business failure rate increased by 60 per cent over the previous year, with collapses running at 1,600 a month compared with 1,000 a month last winter.

(*Independent*, 2 Jan. 1991)

Figure 22.3

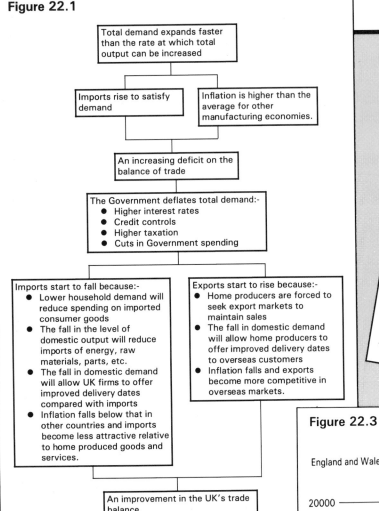

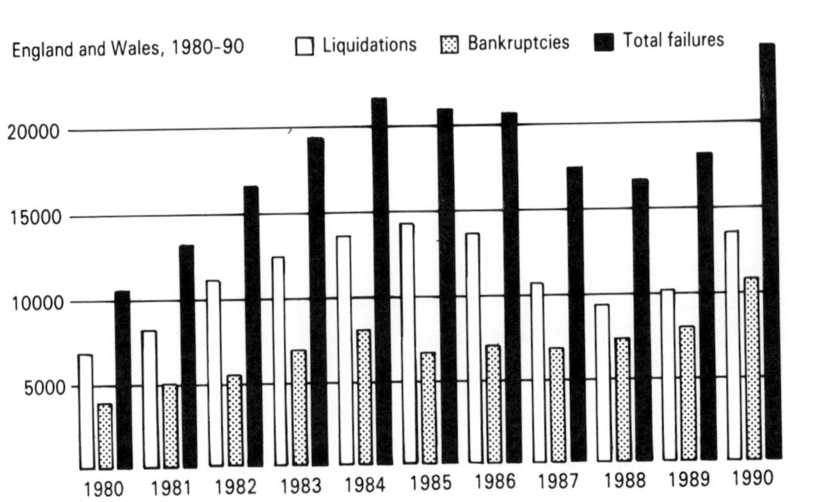

Source: Dun & Bradstreet (*Observer*, 6 Jan. 1991)

Having put the pound into the European exchange rate mechanism the government will find it politically much more difficult to remove the pound from the system and use a lower exchange rate as a means of helping the competitive position of UK producers. It will now have to tackle inflation and trade deficits by deflating the total level of spending in the economy. By depressing market demand in this way the government will hope to create a financial and business climate that will eventually reduce inflationary pressures, curb the growth of imports and encourage exports. The ways in which this kind of policy operates to improve the UK's trading position is outlined in Figure 22.1 above.

Figure 22.4

Trade deficit falls to three-year low

Larry Elliott
Economics Correspondent

BRITAIN's trade deficit fell to its lowest level for three and a half years in the three months to November as imports fell sharply and exports continued to grow.

Figures released by the Central Statistical Office yesterday showed that the onset of recession has led to a marked drop in demand for imported manufactures over the past quarter.

And although exports are no longer growing as quickly as earlier in the year, the slump in the UK car market has stimulated a dramatic increase in overseas orders. The number of cars exported is up 29 per cent on a year ago, while imports are down by 9.5 per cent.

According to the CSO, Britain's trade deficit in manufactures, food and raw materials stood at £971 million last month, down from £1,064 million in October. The figures were broadly in line with City expectations, with both imports and exports little changed.

However, in the three months to November – a better guide to the underlying trend – imports fell by £800 million and exports rose by £1,000 million. As a result, the visible trade gap shrank from £4.6 billion to £2.8 billion, the smallest deficit since the £2.6 billion in the three months to May 1987.

Over the past quarter, the deficit in finished manufactures has fallen by two-thirds to £700 million. Of the £1.4 billion improvement, £1.2 billion was caused by an across the board drop in imports, a sign that recession has weakened the demand for foreign consumer and investment goods.

John Shepperd, analyst with S.G. Warburg, said the evidence that industry was de-stocking meant there was the potential for the improvement to continue early next year.

The curb on imports has also narrowed the UK's enormous trade gap with the rest of the European Community. In the three months to November, the shortfall was £1.6 billion, down from £2.9 billion in the previous three months and £4 billion in the same months last year.

(*Guardian*, 22 Dec. 1990)

Figure 22.5

Boots confirms recession has caught up with less-expensive end of the high street

Ben Laurance

BOOTS the Chemists yesterday became the first big retailer to admit that spending in the run-up to Christmas failed to match the level seen in 1989. The disclosure confirms that the effect of the high street downturn has now moved beyond those retailers selling expensive and luxury items, and has caught up with shops catering to everyday needs.

Yesterday's announcement from Boots indicates that the nature of the consumer squeeze is changing. The first shops to be hit were those whose sales relied heavily on the housing market. These included furniture retailers and shops selling 'white goods' like fridges and cookers. Last year saw the squeeze spread to retailers like clothing shops where consumers can easily put off a purchase until a later date. If the experience of Boots is repeated with other chains catering for basic goods where the average sale price is relatively low, this will indicate that the consumer spending downturn has now entered its third phase.

Economists at Goldman Sachs predict that consumer spending in the first three months of this year after taking off inflation will be 1.7 per cent below its level at the beginning of 1990. But this includes food sales, which are more resilient in any downturn, so the fall in non-food spending is likely to be steeper.

(*Guardian*, 22 Dec. 1990)

Figure 22.6

The first pains of ERM

The combination of yesterday's sharp jump in UK unemployment and the chancellor's earlier refusal to countenance a base rate cut starts to look ominous. Perhaps the ERM – the enforced recession mechanism, as the wags have it – is starting to bite already. In the US, the attempt is being made to duck recession through the time-honoured method of devaluation. The UK government, by contrast, seems inclined to sweat it out.

If yesterday's figures on average earnings are anything to go by, there is more pain to come. Wage inflation seems stuck on the 10 per cent plateau it first reached back in June. Meanwhile unemployment, at 6.2 per cent, is only slightly up from its low of 5.6 per cent in April. Given a fixed exchange rate, the obvious next step is for wage inflation to be forced down by a lengthening dole queue.

(*Financial Times*, 14 Dec. 1990)

Figure 22.7

Economic indicator: CBI industrial trends survey

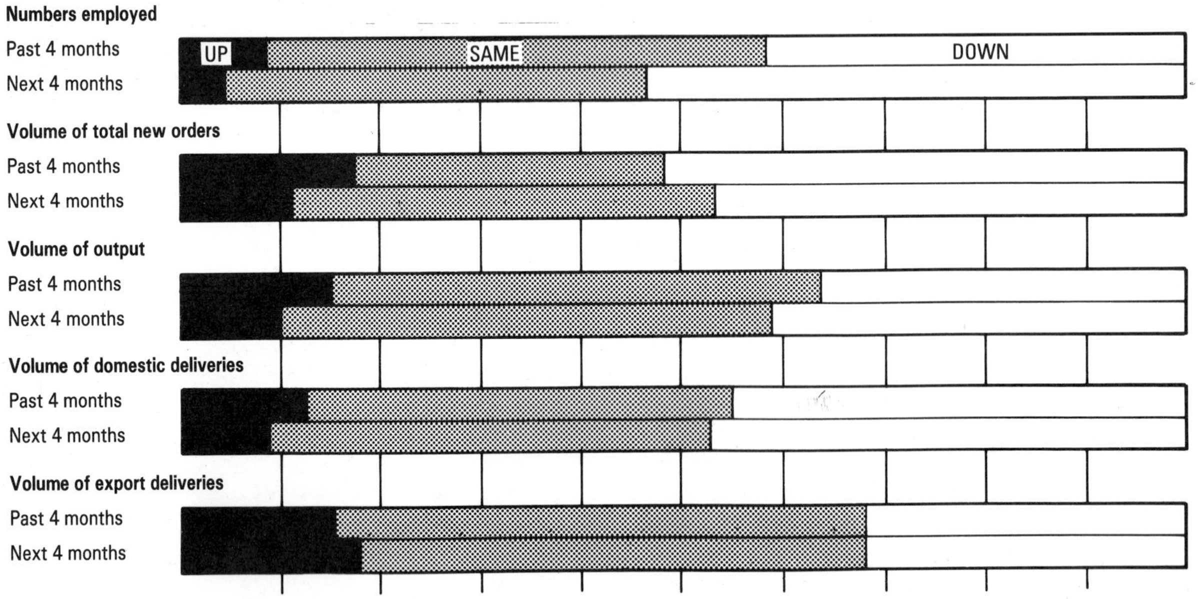

IF THE CBI hasn't persuaded the Government to cut interest rates it's hard to know what will. The CBI's quarterly trends surveys are regarded as an accurate barometer of the state of Britain's industrial heartland. And last week's survey spelt out how bad the recession has become. Business confidence among members has fallen more sharply than at any time since October 1980, investment by manufacturing companies is likely to fall by 16 per cent in the year to mid-1991, 89,000 job losses are expected up to March and 13 per cent of companies predict a fall in export volumes over the next four months. John Major's reply was that interest rates would be reduced 'when it is appropriate to do so'.

(*Observer*, 3 Feb. 1991)

Figure 22.8

(*Independent on Sunday*, 30 Dec. 1990)

Figure 22.9

CBI warns of rise in redundancies

by Michael Harrison

THE CONFEDERATION of British Industry yesterday predicted a flood of redundancies in 1991 unless the latest drop in the size of pay settlements was sustained in the coming months.

The warning came as the employers' organisation reported that pay deals had finally begun to ease back after three years of continuous growth.

According to the CBI's latest pay databank, manufacturing settlements in the third quarter averaged 8.6 per cent compared with 9 per cent in the previous quarter. This is the first time the CBI has reported a drop since the fourth quarter of 1987.

Despite the heartening news on pay the CBI painted a gloomy picture on productivity. The survey shows that growth in output is down to its lowest level for three years.

The manufacturers' estimates in the third quarter measured a productivity improvement in the previous 12 months of 4.5 per cent. To maintain international competitiveness, pay settlements would need to have been contained at no more than two percentage points above productivity growth.

However, only a third of firms achieved this – a trend which points to more redundancies ahead, the CBI warns.

The CBI estimates that as the recession deepens unemployment will rise towards two million by the end of next year. John Banham, the organisation's director general, said: 'The growth in unemployment can only accelerate unless lower pay settlements lead inflation downwards.'

He added that to use the retail price index as a target in pay negotiations would be to put jobs in the firing line. 'If such recklessness prevails there will be needless job losses, bringing bleak prospects to thousands of families in the new year.

'Pay must reflect performance in the boardroom and on the shop floor, in services and manufacturing, in public and private sectors,' he stated.

The CBI's warning came as the public sector unions representing hundreds of thousands of workers gear up to make substantial wage claims next year. Hospital ancillary workers, local government staff and manual staff in the electricity industry are all expected to submit claims above the level of inflation, while railway workers and ambulance men are also drawing up high claims.

In line with the easing of manufacturing pay claims, the CBI survey also suggests that service sector wage demands may also be moderating. Although pay deals within private sector service firms crept up from 8.9 per cent in the first half of 1990 to 9 per cent in the second half of the year, this was below the 9.2 per cent recorded between July and December 1989.

Despite the fall in the size of reported wage settlements there are indications that the trend could return to an upward path in the fourth quarter when the figures will include a rash of double-digit pay rises achieved by car workers at Ford, Vauxhall and Jaguar.

(*Independent*, 28 Dec. 1990)

SHORT-ANSWER QUESTIONS

1. What kinds of firms are most likely to be affected if the government cuts its capital expenditure as part of its policy of reducing the total level of spending in the economy?
2. Distinguish between liquidation and bankruptcies.
3. Why are small firms particularly vulnerable to high interest rates and falling consumer demand?
4. Explain the possible connection between the slump in the UK car market and higher car exports.
5. What kinds of imported consumer goods would you expect to be most affected by the fall in the level of consumer expenditure?
6. Why will a fall in the level of industrial output in the UK always contribute to a reduction in imports?
7. What is the evidence that households are being particularly hard hit by the squeeze on consumer expenditure?
8. Why is it necessary to adjust data on consumer spending by 'taking off inflation'?
9. Why might the reaction of firms to prospects of a recession actually contribute to an even deeper recession?
10. What would have been the most immediate benefits to firms if the government had responded to pressure from the CBI for a significant cut in interest rates?
11. Explain why large pay increases at a time of falling demand were expected to lead to a flood of redundancies.
12. Why might a firm experiencing a fall in output also suffer from a decline in the productivity of labour?

ANALYSING BUSINESS SITUATIONS

1. Discuss the use of regulations that fix the minimum deposit and maximum repayment period on hire-purchase agreements rather than just relying upon higher interest rates as a way of reducing the level of consumer spending.
2. Assess the relationship between interest rates and business failures in the 1980s.
3. What factors could have accounted for the regional variations in the level of business failures?
4. Explain the relationship between house prices, mortgage advances, increases in interest rates and the level of consumer spending.
5. Why would you expect the level of pay settlements to be 'forced down by a lengthening dole queue'?
6. Why should any improvement in the UK's trading position brought about by de-stocking and a fall in investment not be viewed as a 'solution' to the trade deficit?
7. Why will the deflation of total demand oblige firms to pay more attention to their labour costs and avoid price increases?
8. Describe the kinds of developments in the UK economy which are likely to play a major role in depressing the level of business confidence.
9. What were the problems facing employers when seeking to persuade their employees to accept a pay increase of 6 per cent when inflation, although on a downward trend, was still 9.4 per cent? What arguments could these employers have used to support their case for much lower pay settlements?
10. Explain the relationship between interest rates, the housing market and the level of consumer spending. Why will some existing owner-occupiers also be forced to reduce their consumer expenditure?
11. Assess the possible effects of substantial wage increases in the public sector and the motor vehicle industry upon pay claims in other parts of the UK economy.
12. Why might motor vehicle manufacturers in the UK have been in a position to award double-digit pay rises without endangering their competitive position against foreign manufacturers?

ACTIVITIES

LOCAL STUDY

(a) Survey your local area and gather information that relates to closures, openings or expansion of various kinds of retail outlets and other businesses that meet consumer demand such as catering, recreation, entertainment and travel.

(b) Trace what has happened to the banks' base rate and mortgage rate since the end of 1990 and assess the extent to which such changes may have contributed to the kind of developments that you have identified in (a) above.

(c) What other factors may have been responsible for any changes in the level and pattern of consumer spending in your local area?

(d) Take a group of these retail outlets and other businesses and comment on the extent to which they give rise to such imports as consumer goods, materials, parts and equipment.

INVESTIGATION

Investigate what happened to inflation, unemployment and the UK's visible trade balance in the period from January 1991.

ESSAYS

1. (**a**) Explain how changes in interest rates alter opportunity costs for a firm.

(**b**) Identify areas of organizational activity that might be particularly affected by such change. (Cambridge, June 1989)

2. Examine how an enterprise might alter its plans if a prolonged period of heavy unemployment is predicted. (AEB, June 1988)

3. Analyse the strategies available to a firm to enable it to survive a period of recession in its home market. (AEB, Nov. 1987)

4. 'An over-reliance upon a high interest rate policy to tackle inflation and improve the UK's trading position runs the risk of damaging investment. Producers will face higher borrowing costs, sudden and large fluctuations in their markets and a squeeze on their profits. The overall business climate will not be conducive to the higher investment which is the only longterm solution to a lack of international competitiveness'. Explain and comment upon this statement.

Relocation

Figure 23.1

Make a move in the right direction

Provincial centres are selling themselves hard to attract business migrants. **Jim Levi** reports.

IT IS A sad fact of life in these islands that a provincial city like Manchester or Birmingham – despite their undoubted charms – cannot quite get themselves taken seriously on the world stage.

Relegated to the roles of 'also rans' in the race to stage the Olympics in both 1992 and 1996, they seem unable to capture the charisma of the capital city. London – already the cultural, financial and political centre of the UK – might well have beaten even America's Coca-Cola capital, Atlanta, had it deigned to put itself forward as a candidate.

The regions of Britain, shrugging aside their collective inferiority complex, continue to hone their skills in a bid to sell themselves hard to the commercial world and counteract the magnetic power of London and the South-east. If they cannot have as many opera houses and art galleries as London they can invariably boast more Japanese high-tech transplants.

Questions about relocation are becoming more complex and the choice facing any company thinking of making a move is more bewildering. The major concern of companies in the South considering a move is the problem of staff turnover.

This is reflected particularly by financial services companies – banks, insurance companies and the like – moving much of the 'back office' processing work out of London and into regional centres. There have been countless examples of this: Pearl Assurance to Peterborough, Sun Alliance to Bristol, Midland Bank to Sheffield, TSB to Scotland and National Provincial Institution to South Wales.

The pressure to attract and retain 'back office' staff may to some extent lessen with the onset of recession. But the problem of the demographic 'time bomb' – the increasing shortage of school leavers – is unlikely to go away.

In selling itself, a region, a city or a new town may need to stress all kinds of attractions. Good road and rail communications are often the starting point. Potential movers want to know they can easily get back to where they are coming from and to access the markets for their goods and services.

The strength of the M4 corridor as a 'hot spot' in the economy owes much to the combination of the M4 with the high-speed rail link to South Wales. Other regions are anxious to replicate this.

What has happened to Reading, Swindon, Cheltenham, Bristol and South Wales may also happen to Oxford, Banbury, Warwick, and the West Midlands with the opening of the M40 London to Birmingham link.

Faster rail/road connections may also be a major factor in boosting the North-east next year when the London–Newcastle journey time comes down to only two-and-a-half hours.

Financial incentives take the form of basic cost savings such as rents, business rates and salary costs, as well as grants and cheap loans. If getting a grant is the key trigger there is a wide choice of locations in assisted areas. Such grants can bring savings of up to 30 per cent of the cost of moving.

In the end the factor loosely called 'lifestyle' may determine whether and where any organisation relocates. Proximity to the chief executive's favourite golf course is certainly one factor in Scotland's relocation success story. Other regions try hard to match that. Liverpool talks of the great Beatles 'heritage' while up in Geordieland the PR machine offers the counter-attractions of Sting and *Viz* magazine. And of course it remains true that many of Britain's ugliest urban creations of the industrial revolution are surrounded by spectacular countryside.

Reward Group, the Staffordshire-based pay research organisation, has devised its own Quality of Life Index for the regions of Britain.

It was based on comparing the various costs of living and salary levels in the different regions. The index was calculated by taking the average salary of a middle manager in each region and comparing it to the national average and also by comparing the cost of living in the region with the national average.

The result is an index with Scotland at the top showing a quality of life 16.6 per cent above the national average. Greater London ranks last, 21.9 per cent below.

At the end of the day, hard-headed logic ought to prevail. And more often than not it is the achievement of a kind of 'critical mass' of new immigrants into a region that becomes its most attractive feature.

This creates that snowball effect which is the ultimate goal of all the relocation agencies. To some extent it has already been achieved by some regions.

In the North-east for example, the arrival of Nissan in Sunderland almost certainly had some influence on the decision of another Japanese giant, Fujitsu, to locate its first European semiconductor plant on a site in County Durham.

And Milton Keynes, with no financial inducements, now has the pulling power to draw in new companies at the rate of three a week. It boasts a tally of nearly 40 Japanese companies.

In South Wales the inward investment begun by Sony led to other Japanese consumer electronics companies moving in.

The arrival in that region of dozens of foreign firms encouraged the Welsh Development Agency to push for expansion of financial services companies.

The AA started the ball rolling a decade ago by moving its insurance services to Cardiff. It has since been followed by Chemical Bank, TSB, National Provident, Rothschilds and Lloyds Bank.

(*Observer*, 3 Aug. 1990)

Figure 23.2

Capital punishment, regional rewards

London rents have eased but businesses are still rushing North in search of better surroundings. **David Lawson** reports.

'WHEN a man is tired of London,' said Johnson, 'he is tired of life.' Two centuries on, the familiar words still have a plausible ring. The undoubted attractions of Britain's primary city continue to suck in people, power and money.

On the other hand there is always a steady trickle of people and businesses away from the capital, driven out by high costs or lack of space to expand. In the 1990s the trickle may become a torrent.

Despite the property crash, office space in the City or the West End still costs almost three times as much as its equivalent in Birmingham, Bristol or Leeds.

Tenants will normally endure higher rents provided profits are rising and there is suitable space to expand. In the late 1980s, however, rents began to surge, and even profitable firms started to feel the pinch. In addition, staff disenchanted with crowded roads and soaring rail fares were deserting in droves or demanding more money. Tenants faced with high rents and wage demands had to reassess their position. A move to cheaper, older property was not an option – the computer technology found in even the humblest of modern businesses demands newer premises.

Last year 7,000 jobs were moved out of London, and, according to Mike Koudra of property consultancy Jones Lang Wootton, plans are in place for at least another 20,000 up to 1992. Even though the downturn in the economy has slashed rents in London and opened up acres of empty space in new office buildings the exodus shows no sign of abating.

Advanced technology and increasing environmental demands are the main reasons for this break with the past. Firms linked via computer screens realise they can survive north of Watford. And staff are demanding more of life than Dr Johnson's congested paradise.

Moves in the 1990s aim for better buildings in pleasant surroundings rather than merely an escape from higher rents.

Even the slump in house prices has not discouraged firms determined to leave. Jim McCredie at KPMG Peat Marwick McLintock, which handles some 20 corporate moves a year, reassured one client aiming to keep a third of its 700 staff in a move to the Midlands that bridging finance would add only £1 million to its costs. This paled into insignificance against the £11 million KPMG estimated the company would save over 20 years by moving from the South-east.

Until recently London companies relocating rarely ventured far, settling into places like the Thames Valley. But these areas have become victims of their own success, with jostling newcomers boosting rents and soaking up local staff. McCredie has grave doubts whether some firms making short-distance moves saved much at all. As well as all the costs of the move they would have met similar high wage rates, expensive houses and scarcity of staff.

Recent studies suggest that regional centres more than 100 miles from London are now in favour. First Bristol and Birmingham, then Manchester, Leeds and Newcastle have tasted a regional 'renaissance' as expansion rippled northwards. Foreign companies looking for a toehold in Europe are also opting for the regions.

This renaissance helped prime rents to soar by 25 per cent last year in the North and Midlands, compared with just 2 per cent in the South-east.

But although rents may ease in the South, congestion and labour shortages will not go away. London's transport investment plans barely scratch the surface and workers' aspirations for a better environment will ensure that the drain from the metropolis continues.

This does not mean London will become a ghost town: it can afford to lose far more than 20,000 jobs every couple of years and still maintain its pre-eminence.

But office tenants and their staff are discovering that London does not hold all that life can offer, and a new world beckons north of Watford.

Konnichiwa, Milton Keynes

Case study NYK Line

A NEW Japanese-built cruiseliner, Crystal Harmony, enters service in 1991 but it will be provisioned from Milton Keynes – arguably the most inland city in Britain. The example illustrates how geography is much less important than it used to be when it comes to relocating a business. One of Japan's oldest shipping lines, NYK Line, part of the massive Mitsubishi trading group, decided to set up shop in Milton Keynes for a number of reasons. Not least was the fact that the Japanese industrial community in the city is already sizeable, with a total of 37 companies. There is even a private school for Japanese children. But NYK also found communication links good enough to site its new European operations centre there.

NYK, though now one of the largest shipping companies in the world, has diversified into land and air transport, so proximity to port facilities has become less important than having the right communications links. Even so, it is surprising that NYK did not choose somewhere like Rotterdam. That city will doubtless follow as NYK expands its European interests, but the decision to go to Milton Keynes first is, as much as anything, down to the fact that the Japanese feel more comfortable dealing in English than in any other European language.

(*Observer*, 30 Aug. 1990)

Figure 23.3

Taking the high road, loch, stock and barrel

Low costs and a skilled workforce make Scotland a prime location for expanding industries. Jim Levi reports.

DAVID BROWN is typical of the new breed of relocation professionals striving to get the last ounce of competitive advantage for the region they serve.

His patch is the whole of Scotland, a region with four Enterprise Zones and more than half its land mass covered by Government financial assistance schemes.

Brown learned his craft in Stamford, Connecticut where he was part of the Locate in Scotland team who promote the country to potential outside investors for the Scottish Development Agency.

His four-year US apprenticeship ended some two years ago when he took charge of the agency's London office. Now the marketing techniques applied in Connecticut are being put to good effect in London.

'We make extensive use of information technology. While we were in Stamford we covered the whole of the American east coast, and we developed our own programme to identify all US companies selling into the European market which had no manufacturing presence there,' he explains. 'We were then able systematically to approach all of those companies and tell them about the merits of Scotland.'

That same comprehensive approach is now being tried in the South-east of England. 'We reckon 80 per cent of companies who relocate are not uprooting the entire company. They are seeking expansion and their growth is being constrained in some way,' he says.

'We have identified all the companies in the South-east we think would be of interest to us.'

As far as Brown is concerned that includes a range of industries already well established north of the Border. They include financial services, advanced engineering, electronics hardware and software and healthcare.

'We have to look at projects through the eyes of the companies we are trying to persuade to move,' says Brown. 'We make the approach and set about convincing the directors that it would be in their interests to expand in Scotland.'

The concentration is very much on the bottom line with Brown claiming that a typical 30,000 sq ft office with say 200 people could save the company as much as £3 million a year if transferred from central London to Glasgow or Edinburgh.

'Golf and sailing may have their attractions but it is numbers like these that really count,' he says. 'Only by being able to produce models of the kind of cost savings which can be achieved can we get the vital element of credibility that we need.'

And of course it is cost savings on this scale which are going to be very appealing to any company fearing the consequences of an industrial recession.

Any fears of being too remote from the market-place may well be exaggerated. Zonal, a company based near Gatwick airport, found it tough to recruit technical staff to produce its high quality recording tape for broadcasting companies around the world.

So, managing director Alfred Heise relocated to Invergordon near Inverness where the main source of employment – an aluminium smelting plant – was closed down some years ago. Zonal now says that it can transport its products from Invergordon to Heathrow almost as cheaply as it could from the old factory at Redhill.

Typical of Brown's pro-active approach is his project to build up an aircraft refurbishment operation at Prestwick for international airlines – to provide what the aerospace industry calls 'deep maintenance'.

'There is a huge skill shortage in the aerospace industry, estimated at about 140,000 engineers worldwide,' he says. 'Our solution is to try to bring the aircraft to where the skills are – in Scotland.'

He reckons there are some 500 such suitably skilled engineers in Ayrshire alone.

For the financial services industry Scotland's already established financial community in Edinburgh, Glasgow, Perth and Dundee is a particular attraction to those who might otherwise fear their career patterns would be upset by a move from London.

Equally, when companies such as TSB Home Loans move to Glasgow they are agreeably surprised by the volume and quality of applications from people already thoroughly familiar with the financial services market.

In the same way, there are encouraging signs that the higher technology engineering and electronics industry is now so well entrenched in Scotland that companies are even relocating their research and development operations there. Rediffusion Simulators in Crawley, for example, decided to switch its software design operations to Glenrothes. Indeed, it was back in the mid-Seventies that Digital, the computer company, first put a semi-conductor research facility into Scotland.

'We are trying very hard to shift companies in Scotland further up the research and development spectrum,' declares Brown.

He believes the performance of the education system in Scotland is the long-term key to attracting more technology-based businesses there. And he will happily show you a table contrasting the achievement rates of Scottish school-leavers with those in England and Wales over the past 10 years.

Latest figures suggest that 18 per cent of Scottish men and 22 per cent of Scottish women leave school with three or more Scottish Higher Certificate passes; in England and Wales, by contrast, the equivalent of two or more 'A' levels are achieved by only 13 per cent of men and women.

Swiss partners for Highland fling

Case study Schindler Lifts

THE shortage of suitably qualified graduates in both Germany and Switzerland prompted Schindler Lifts to expand its research and development operations to Livingston, in Scotland. This international manufacturer of lifts and escalators is spending £500,000 on its new R&D facility – the first of its kind the company has built outside its headquarters at Ebikon in Switzerland. The Livingston centre will take on about 20 specialist software engineers. They will be experienced in the use of advanced computer software and artificial intelligence techniques to develop new applications. Initially the centre will work on projects originating in Switzerland, but before long it is expected to be producing its own new generation of products for the company. 'Schindler has found a ready source of high quality software and computer science graduates in Scotland,' says Gordon Aitken of the Scottish Development Agency. He believes that the demographic pressures throughout continental Europe will make it increasingly difficult for high-tech companies such as Schindler to find and retain the right calibre of staff. 'We expect other Swiss and German firms to take advantage of Scottish skills. We now have eight universities producing computer graduates of the highest quality.'

(*Observer*, 30 Aug. 1990)

SHORT-ANSWER QUESTIONS

1. What locational factors contribute to the 'magnetic power of London and the South-East'?
2. Why did companies in the South face a particularly high rate of staff turnover?
3. What are the problems associated with a high staff turnover?
4. What factors contribute to differences in the costs of living between various regions of the UK?
5. Explain how the attraction of certain kinds of firms to an area may eventually produce a 'snowball' effect.
6. Why will traffic congestion increase a firm's costs?
7. Describe the role played by bridging finance in helping employees to move to a new location. What other kinds of action can a firm take to help employees to relocate?
8. Why might the advantages of relocation a short distance from London prove to be only temporary?
9. Why do the various Development Agencies place so much emphasis upon attracting foreign companies?
10. What factors make the UK in general and certain regions in particular an attractive location for foreign companies?
11. To what extent do some regions of the UK have an image problem when seeking to attract firms currently located in the South?
12. What are the general characteristics of assisted areas?
13. What are the advantages to a company of locating in an Enterprise Zone?

ANALYSING BUSINESS SITUATIONS

1. Explain the part played by advances in information technology in the decision of a company to seek new premises.
2. Describe the various aspects of the physical and social environment which can play an important role in influencing decisions on relocation.
3. Explain what is meant by 'back office' processing work in relation to financial services. Why does this kind of work tend to be very 'footloose' in terms of location?
4. Why is the demographic 'time bomb' of particular concern to the financial services sector?
5. What kinds of companies are likely to be influenced by faster rail connections when considering a new location? What aspects of their business will benefit from shorter rail-journey times?
6. Describe the different ways in which both an economic boom and an economic recession can exert pressure upon a company to relocate.
7. Outline the reasons why Lloyds Bank moved a large part of its operations out of London. Why did Bristol prove to be an attractive area for their relocation?

ACTIVITIES

LOCAL STUDY

(a) Identify those companies which have moved into your area over the last few years.
(b) Contact some of these companies and obtain information on the kinds of products, processes or services which they are involved in and the number of people they employ.
(c) Assess the relative importance of the locational factors which may have attracted these companies to your area and the particular sites which they occupy.
(d) Design a quarter-page advertisement which is to be carried by the national quality newspapers to highlight the locational advantages offered by your area.

ESSAYS

1. To what extent is the availability of such facilities as good restaurants, schools and golf-courses a more important locational factor for modern hi-tech industry than any of the conventional factors? (AEB, Nov. 1987)
2. Why is it becoming possible for manufacturing businesses to be less geographically concentrated than in the past? (AEB, Nov. 1988)
3. (a) Do entrepreneurs always aim to minimize average costs when deciding on a location for a new factory?
(b) Identify other factors which might influence the decision and explain difficulties which are likely to arise in reaching such a decision. (University of Cambridge, June 1988)

Monopolies and mergers

Figure 24.1

Attack on a complex monopoly

By Christopher Parkes, Consumer Industries Editor

THE MONOPOLIES and Mergers Commission yesterday published a critical and weighty report designed to crush the complex monopoly which it has found at work in the British brewing industry.

Focusing on the six national brewers, the commission ranged beyond its basic brief to investigate the supply of beer, and found restrictions on choice, hostility to would-be competitors and distortions of trade wherever it looked: in pricing, in tenancy arrangements, the supply of soft drinks, spirits, cider and low-alcohol beers.

Allied Breweries, the Allied-Lyons subsidiary, Bass, Courage, Grand Metropolitan, Scottish & Newcastle and Whitbread will all be affected by the recommendation that no brewer should own more than 2,000 on-licenced premises. Bass faces the biggest task in disposing of 5,300 while Scottish & Newcastle has to sell only 300.

In arriving at the 2,000 figure, the commission noted that the measure would not affect regional or local brewers. The figure was big enough, it said, for the brewers to employ plant of an economic size especially since the pubs kept would probably be the largest. They would also be able to keep up volumes through greater sales to the free trade.

The other main recommendations were:

- A ban on the granting of tied loans, under which brewers offer owners of free houses substantial loans at low interest rates on condition that they stock specified quantities of the lenders' products.

The commission discovered that loan-tied houses accounted for more than 25 per cent of the national brewers' total beer sales. 'This seriously restricts the opportunities open to the smaller brewers to expand their business,' the report said, as well as limiting customer choice.

- An end to restrictions, commonly imposed by brewers, such as product ties and controls over the future use of pubs which are sold. The commission rejected Brewers' Society claims that a tie, obliging a new owner to stock specific products, effectively reduced the price of the pub, thus easing a newcomer's entry to the trade. 'The proprietor . . . is restricted in the choice he can offer consumers and may be purchasing beer at a price which will give him little opportunity to price his products competitively,' the commission said.

Although the Brewers' Society said its members had almost entirely ceased imposing covenants on sold pubs, forcing the new owners to use them for other purposes, the commission still recommended a formal ban on the practice.

- Tied tenants should be protected by the Landlord and Tenant Act. The brewers told the commission that tenancies, which account for about 53 per cent of their beer sales, provided opportunities for individuals to run their own businesses. However, the commission found that restrictions on the tenants' freedom of action meant that the relationship between brewer and tenant was much closer to that of employer and employee.

Tenants' representatives told the commission that they felt considerable constraint and were under pressure in some cases to buy all their drinks from the brewer. The tenants believed that if they did not, they would be labelled 'poor company men' and their premises would receive less investment and modernisation. Failure to toe the line could also lead to higher rents.

- Tied tenants should be free to buy low-alcohol or alcohol-free beers, wines, spirits, ciders, soft drinks, water and cider from the most competitive suppliers. The commission rejected brewers' claims that customers had a wide selection to choose from in their pubs. Guinness, the stout maker which owns no pubs, Bulmers, the cider maker, and Coca-Cola Schweppes Beverages (CCSB) and others provided evidence to convince the commission that the brewers, not the customers, decided which products should be supplied.

Bulmers complained that it has lost market share through the rapid and systematic exclusion of its ciders from pubs.

The soft drinks market was similarly affected by the reorganisation that took place during the two-and-a-half year commission probe. It involved the formation of Britvic Corona under the control of Bass with minority stakes held by Allied and Whitbread. The company supplies Pepsi-Cola and Britvic fruit juices. 'It now appears that companies owning Britvic Corona are excluding the products of CCSB from the managed estates and to some degree also from their tenanted estates,' the report found.

- Brewers should publish and adhere to wholesale price lists, the commission said, showing prices and discounts available to all customers. They should also be obliged to encourage the development of an independent drinks wholesaling network with a requirement to supply such companies from their breweries or depots at a price which took into account the saving on the brewers' distribution costs.

Some wholesalers had complained that the discounts they were offered were lower than those offered to some retail outlets. The commission concluded: 'We are convinced . . . that the reason why most brewers are at best neutral and at worst hostile to independent wholesalers is the threat that they perceive would arise to their own wholesaling and retailing activities if a strong independent wholesaling force came into being.'

The brewers were also judged to have used the complex monopoly to impose price increases on beer. Since 1979 the price of a pint of bitter, excluding VAT and excise duties, had risen by 15 per cent more than the rate of general inflation measured by the Retail Prices Index. Wholesale beer prices also rose by a real 15 per cent between 1981 and 1986.

The brewers drew attention to the cost of heavy investment in pub improvements, suggesting increases were needed to finance them. But the commission said it did not consider that improvements to public house amenities had been much greater than in retailing generally. 'Moreover, improvement in retail amenity cannot explain increases in the retail price of beer,' it added.

The commission was also critical of the brewers' pricing policies on lager, which commonly sells for about 10p a pint more than ale. Dismissing claims of heavy advertising budgets and higher direct costs than in ale production, the commission found that some brewers' production costs for lager were actually lower than those for other beers.

Lager had represented over 25 per cent of the UK beer market for the last 10 years, and now makes up nearly 50 per cent of the total. 'The price differential can no longer be justified on the grounds that it is a new product,' the report said.

(*Financial Times*, 22 March 1989)

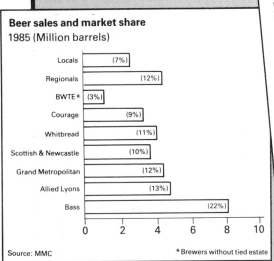

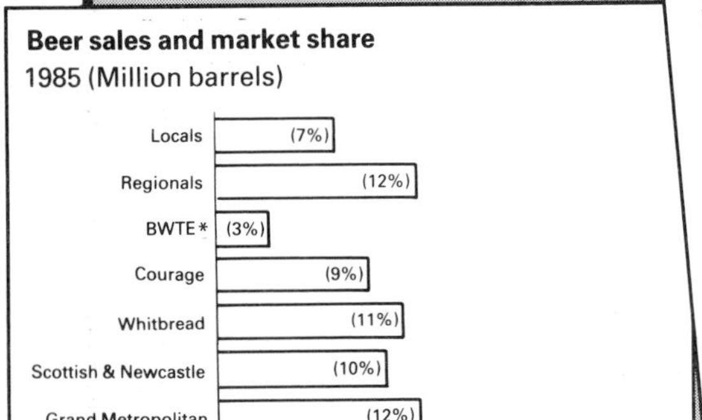

Figure 24(b)

'No decent excuse' for beer increases

James Erlichman, Consumer Affairs Correspondent

An increase in beer prices of 7p a pint, imposed this week by Allied Breweries, makers of Tetley, Burton and Ind Coope ales, takes the price of a pint to above £1.50 in most parts of London.

The rise follows one imposed two weeks ago by Bass, makers of Bass Worthington, and Tennents, which put up prices in the West Midlands by 7p, and is likely to be followed by a 10p increase from Courage.

Pub attendances are down slightly on last year, but price increases have insured that takings are rising faster than inflation.

Andrew Sangster, spokesman for the Campaign for Real Ale, said: "There is no decent excuse for these rises. Most companies respond in a recession by lowering prices to attract customers. The brewers put prices up while pub attendances are still going down."

Camra claims that most brewers used the Chancellor's budget increases on excise duty and VAT as a fig leaf to boost their prices higher than was required.

City analysts offered "no comment" on whether the big six brewers might be engaged in an informal cartel.

Colin Davies, a brewing analyst with Barclays de Zoete Wedd, said: "Most pubgoers are not interested in the price they pay for a pint. You must remember that pub amenities are far better now than 20 years ago, when spit and sawdust were the rule. People are paying for that in higher beer prices, which are, in effect, the entry fee to a nicer place to be."

Mike Ripley, for the Brewers' Society, said: "The rise in beer prices does reflect the investment that has gone into pubs at the retail end."

The real price of beer (compared with wages) had fallen. "Treasury figures show it took the average man 16 minutes to earn a pint in 1970 and only 12 minutes in 1990."

In 1971, the average price of a pint of bitter in a pub was 12p.

Since 1978 the retail price index for all goods has risen by 252 per cent. By the same measure food has risen by only 207 per cent, but beer has risen by 320 per cent.

The Monopolies and Mergers Commission has not examined beer prices directly. It did conclude in 1989 that the brewers were operating a "complex monopoly" which stifled competition.

The brewers were ordered to allow their publicans to sell a "guest" beer from a competitor, and the MMC also required the brewers to shed thousands of tied pubs.

The latter measure was watered down by the Government, and there have been reports that brewers have used threats to discourage publicans from stocking guest beers.

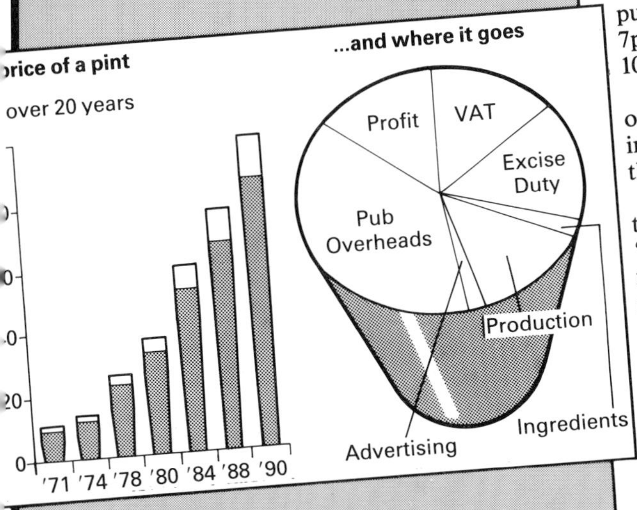

Figure 24(c)

Market shares of largest brewer in each of six EC countries:

Estimates: Barclays de Zoete Wedd, 1990

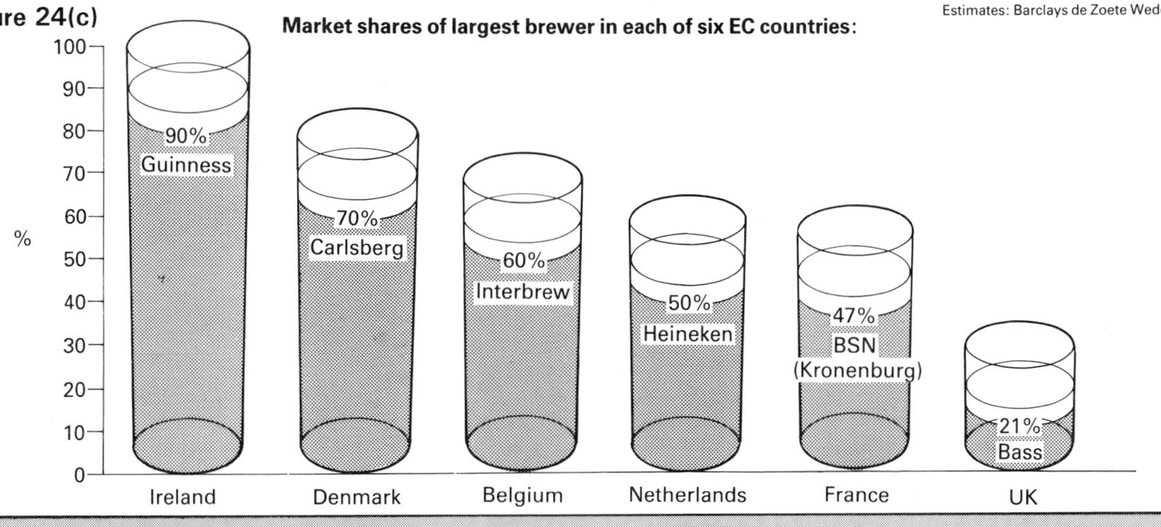

Figure 24(d)

"No head on MMC report"

by Peter Wyles

Criticisms of the MMC's argument

Critics of the MMC pointed out that, whatever the theoretical arguments for or against the existing arrangements, the end result worked reasonably well in practice. While tied houses tend to sell plenty of beers from one brewery only, there are many breweries, and plenty of pubs to choose between.

Britain has the second lowest concentration of brewery ownership in the EC. (The lowest concentration is in Germany, which has a beer industry as fragmented as Britain several decades ago.)

Britain has over a thousand different brands of beer available. The only countries with comparable choice are Germany and Belgium, countries which also have a system of brewers owning pubs.

Nor does the tied house hold out foreign competitors. Britain has the largest number of imported beers available of any European country.

Countries with few tied houses have much more restricted beer markets. Denmark, Holland and Ireland are dominated by Carlsberg, Heineken and Guinness respectively. The tied house was abolished in Australia in 1979 and now two companies have more than 95 per cent of the beer market between them.

Arguments about comparisons of price and choice between different countries flounder because of very different drinking cultures, expected amenities and local laws. For example, a Belgian café will have waiter service, will stay open until the small hours of the morning and may serve food until late at night. This is a different mix of facilities from a British pub.

However, the international evidence does not suggest that the British customer gets a particularly raw deal in terms of the choice on offer:

Criticisms of the MMC's Proposals

Pub Sales

The MMC decided that brewing beer was more profitable than running pubs. But within the brewery industry, it is widely held that running pubs is the more profitable business. Besides which, the value of the brewers' tied estates is far larger than the value of their brewing businesses.

Most of Britain's large brewers said that, given the choice, they would sell off their breweries to other companies, rather than lose control of their pubs. The most likely buyers of these large breweries would have been large foreign breweries, like Anheuser Busch of America, who want to enter the European beer market. Pubs would have remained owned by the same companies as at present.

There would have been massive rationalisation of breweries and brands among the larger breweries. Fewer, larger brewers would have promoted their national brands more heavily, which would have made competition more difficult for smaller companies.

The large brewers said that if somehow they were forced to sell thousands of pubs, it would disrupt the lives of their tenants and it would lead to the closure of many of the less profitable pubs – for example, those in remote rural areas. The brewers said that many pubs were only viable within the tied house system.

Loans to free houses and clubs

The proposal to ban loans to free houses and clubs was criticised, because brewers say they are often prepared to loan money where banks were not. The brewers argued that loans were of great benefit to small free houses and clubs, providing necessary cash for refurbishment and better facilities. Ending loans would have meant lower standards, and perhaps fewer free houses starting up.

Tenant security

The proposals to strengthen tenant security alarmed many of the traditional regional brewers. They felt very strongly that they would no longer be able to control who ran their pubs, a business which they owned and which was their 'public face'.

The guest beer

The guest beer was also of concern to many of the regional brewers. All the regional brewers told the MMC that they needed their tied estates to compete against the national brewers.

The regional brewers felt that with the guest beer, tenants of all companies would take heavily advertised and heavily discounted national brands. The marketing power of the larger brewers would ensure that the small brewers would lose a lot of trade in their own pubs – probably far more than the guest beer trade they could gain from other people.

If the larger brewers were forced to leave brewing, because of the 2,000 pub limit, their pub estates would remain closed to the local brewers. The guest beer would not have applied to these non-brewing companies.

Peter Wyles is a journalist who followed the MMC report and subsequent developments for various publications covering the brewing industry.

SHORT-ANSWER QUESTIONS

1. What is the role of (a) the Monopolies and Mergers Commission (MMC) and (b) the Office of Fair Trading?
2. Why do you think that there was a case for the MMC to investigate the brewing industry?
3. Under what circumstances might 'free houses' be such in name only?
4. Outline some of the possible sources of economies associated with horizontal and vertical integration in the brewing industry.
5. What factors are likely to encourage a brewer to merge with or take over a major producer of soft drinks or spirits?
6. What is meant by a rise in the 'real' price of beer?
7. Why did the MMC not propose that brewers should dispose of all their pubs as a way of encouraging greater competition?
8. Explain why the weakening of the tie for tenanted houses could affect a brewer's plans to invest in its retail outlets.
9. Why did the brewers claim that many rural pubs would be forced to close down?
10. Why did the MMC propose that tied tenants should be given greater security in their relationships with the companies that owned their premises?
11. What factors may have been responsible for draught lager taking a larger share of the market at the expense of other kinds of beer?

ANALYSING BUSINESS SITUATIONS

1. Why did the MMC see the sale of brewery-owned retail outlets and the removal of 'tied loans' as a way of encouraging greater price competition and wider consumer choice?
2. What is meant by 'plant of an economic size' and how did the capital-intensive nature of the brewing industry influence the MMC's recommendations on the maximum number of licensed premises that should be owned by a single brewery?
3. How were brewers said to protect themselves from potential competition when disposing of premises which sold their products?
4. How can the influence exerted by the major brewers limit the potential impact of advertising campaigns for Guinness stout, Bulmers cider, Coca-Cola and Schweppes soft drinks?
5. To what extent does the continued growth of large supermarket chains contribute to greater price competition and consumer choice in both alcoholic and non-alcoholic drinks?
6. Between 1968 and 1988 the number of brewing companies fell by nearly 50 per cent. The six major companies now account for 75 per cent of beer sales and own 75 per cent of tied houses. Comment on the view that the interests of consumers would have been better protected if the MMC had controlled mergers and takeovers in previous years.
7. Explain the possible effects upon prices and consumer choice if the major brewers responded by keeping their pubs and selling off their brewing interests.
8. Assess the extent to which tied loans to free houses and clubs may actually widen rather than restrict consumer choice in terms of leisure activities.
9. The Brewers Society responded to the MMC's comment on prices by pointing out that in real terms beer prices in the UK were lower than in many other European countries. To what exent does this make UK beer prices more reasonable?
10. Assume that a reduction in the proportion of brewery-owned pubs produces a fall in the wholesale price of beer as brewers seek to supply such outlets. To what extent do you believe that pubs would then take advantage of this to lower their prices when competing for business?
11. Discuss the view that a brewer would not make a cheap or interest free loan to a club or free house unless it was in their financial interest to do so.
12. The MMC's report also recommended that all tied tenants should be allowed to sell a 'guest' draught beer from another company.

(a) Explain the reasoning behind this proposal.
(b) Why might such a proposal operate against the interests of the small regional brewers?

13. To what extent do you believe that a managed or tied pub or restaurant is justified in charging more for its drinks on the grounds that it helps to finance improvements to the premises?
14. Discuss the view that the tied system encourages brewers to compete with each other on the basis of the improvements which they make to their tenanted pubs and other outlets.

ACTIVITIES

LOCAL STUDY

Design a questionnaire to determine the extent to which the average consumer would be influenced by the following factors when making a choice between pubs:

- significantly lower average prices
- a wider choice of beers/lager on offer
- convenient to home/place of work
- decor, furnishings and fittings
- personality of bar staff
- the type of people who generally use the pub
- games facilities
- music/entertainment
- garden
- value for money food
- facilities for children
- generally not too busy
- ease of parking
- overall atmosphere

The questionnaire should also seek to obtain opinions on the extent to which consumers believe that the pubs in their area currently offer a sufficiently wide range of choice in terms of overall value for money. Use your findings to comment on the degree to which the MMC's proposals would make a significant contribution to the interests of consumers.

ROLE PLAY

Conduct a meeting to discuss the various issues raised by the MMC. Students should act as representatives of the following groups or organizations:

(a) national brewers;
(b) local or regional brewers;
(c) pub tenants;
(d) sports and social clubs;
(e) a consumers' association;
(f) Guinness stout;
(g) Bulmers cider;
(h) Coca-Cola Schweppes beverages.

The growth of Ratners

Figure 25.1

Group structure in the UK

Average transaction values

Ratners	£ 18
H Samuel	£ 25
Zales/Ernest Jones	£ 50
Salisburys	£ 7
Watches of Switzerland	£950

The jewellery market is now one of the major UK retail markets with an annual turnover of more than £2.7 billion. Recent growth has been dramatic, with the market having more than doubled in the past five years. This growth has been driven by the Ratners Group which has fundamentally changed the retailing of jewellery by making it both fashionable and affordable. This powerful combination has taken our market share of specialist jewellery retailers to 31% and it is still growing.

In this developing market three broad segments have emerged; a fashion and low price-orientated market; a broad jewellery, watch and gift mid-market; and a finer quality middle to upper market. In Ratners, H Samuel and Zales/Ernest Jones, the Group provides a focused retail format that dominates each of these market segments.

The Ratners chain with 238 stores at the lower end of the market will continue to provide highly fashionable jewellery at unbeatable prices. H Samuel has 419 stores offering a broader range of jewellery and gift merchandise and appeals to all ages. The strategic acquisition of Zales in 1988 and its subsequent merger with Ernest Jones was most important for the Group. It is this new combined chain that is attacking the upper middle market with its range of diamond jewellery and quality branded watches such as Rolex, Omega and Cartier. This is the area of the jewellery market where the independent retailer still predominates.

The Group has not neglected the very top of the market. We have a small group of shops under the Watches of Switzerland name selling top quality timepieces with agencies including Ebel, Patek Philippe, Rolex and Audemars Piguet.

Our Salisburys chain complements our mainstream jewellery businesses. In addition to its costume jewellery and fashion accessory ranges, Ratners has developed and updated Salisburys former core markets of gifts, handbags and luggage.

There are 1,150 outlets in the British Isles

Ratners	238
H Samuel	419
Zales/Ernest Jones	19
Salisburys	21
Watches of Switzerland	[illegible]
Other	[illegible]

Figure 25.2

Chairman's statement

I am delighted to report that 1989 was another year of significant growth for the Group despite a difficult retailing environment. Pre-tax profits increased by 41% to £121.5 million on sales up 41% at £898.1 million. Fully diluted earnings per share improved by 14% to 30.2p. A proposed final ordinary dividend of 7.5p will bring the total for the year to 9.5p, an increase of 27%.

The Group now has a broad profit base across both the UK and US markets. The US now accounts for approximately 30% of the Group's operating profits, contributing some £38.4 million, an increase of 49%. Sales in the US increased by 47% (7% on a like-for-like basis in dollar terms). It is less than three years since the Group entered the US market through the acquisition of Sterling. Since our entry, our US stores have grown from 117 to 471, our market share has increased from 0.5% to approximately 2.5%. More importantly, the operating profits of Sterling have increased from $14.4 million in the year prior to the acquisition to $62.0 million in 1989. This result includes a modest contribution from Weisfield's which was acquired in December 1989 for $62.1 million in cash.

We have now established a firm competitive edge in the US through superior sourcing and bulk purchasing capabilities enhanced by our UK purchasing requirements. Allied to our advanced merchandising and retailing systems, this should enable us to achieve our medium term objective of 10% of the US jewellery market.

In the UK operating profits increased by 37% to £91.1 million. The Group's long held policy of offering the consumer outstanding value for money along with a continual flow of new and exciting products has helped us achieve this excellent result, despite a difficult economic climate. This was reflected in the sales increases achieved across the Group's jewellery businesses; H Samuel 28%, Ratners 29%, Zales 28%, and Watches of Switzerland 24%. This strength is further highlighted in the strong sales growth coming from the like-for-like space (i.e. sales growth from the same space as last year, excluding additional space acquired), where sales growth was 18% for both H Samuel and Ratners, 24% for Zales and 22% for Watches of Switzerland.

The new headquarters for Ratners and Zales in Colindale, North London has enabled us to replace stock even faster – vital when so much business is done over the Christmas period – and

Figure 25.2 (continued)

gives us significant potential for reducing overheads as a result of combining these two businesses in one building.

This was our first full year of trading with Zales and Salisburys, acquired in November 1988. Zales has been merged with Ernest Jones creating nearly 200 shops. Whilst retaining its position at a market level noticeably above H Samuel and Ratners, we have completely revamped the Zales/Ernest Jones businesses. Ratners stock replenishment systems have been introduced and the shops now offer a new range of merchandise from totally new displays. Consequently, we have strengthened our market share in diamonds and more expensive watches.

We have now successfully implemented our policy of segmenting the market into three distinct profiles. With Watches of Switzerland aiming at the very top end of the market, and Salisburys as our outlet for costume jewellery, we are now represented in all the market segments. This puts us in a strong position to achieve our goal of 50% of the UK jewellery market, which is growing much faster than any other area of the High Street. Whilst Zales has produced immediate and substantial profit increases, Salisburys is taking longer to produce satisfactory returns. Significant investment has been required to bring this business up to the efficiency of the rest of the Group – EPOS is being introduced to all shops, the shops now have greater densities of stock which is distributed frequently, and Ratners retailing systems have been implemented. These factors, combined with better salary structures, have already led to improved staff morale and resulted in a much better sales performance at Salisburys – the second half like-for-like sales increased by 15% against a decrease in the first half of the financial year. This improvement is continuing.

Figure 25.3

Group strategic review: buying

The last five years have seen a fundamental shift in the relationship between retailers and suppliers in the jewellery market. The consolidation of 31% of the turnover of UK specialist jewellers into the Ratners Group has shifted the balance of power towards the retailer and away from the suppliers.

We have used this power to pass on the benefits of bulk purchasing to our customers, giving them even better value for money.

When this strength in the UK is combined with the expertise of Sterling in the US, particularly in diamond buying, the Group has formidable global buying clout. However, the Group's success is not just built on lower prices. Our skills in product selection provide attractive ranges of jewellery that people want to buy.

The task of our buyers is to put together collections of jewellery that complement each other on a display pad. These pads are then assembled into an integrated range that is appropriate to the relevant store format in terms of fashion and price points. The range is then purchased so as to achieve targeted gross margins.

This stringent procedure is followed in both the US and the UK. In both markets though, the process is made easier by very advanced information systems. Our sales history databases, gathered through the extensive use of EPOS equipment, are comprehensive and enable us to model future demand for products and ranges with a high degree of predictability.

Figure 25.4

Group strategic review: stores and systems

"The quality of the Ratners Group stores' positions is generally very high. H Samuel in particular occupy some of the best locations of any retailers on the UK High Streets" – Healey & Baker. Jewellery retailing requires prime High Street footage with good customer traffic but having good sites is, in itself, not enough. Strong rental inflation in the late 1980s has meant that sales footage has to be worked hard in order to keep profits growing. Our retail operations departments seek to maximise sales from the Group's footage. We are pleased to report that in the period ended 3 February 1990, average sales per square foot in our UK jewellery businesses increased to £700 from £590 in the previous year.

At Ratners our estates and operations departments work together to establish the local market requirements. We then ensure that we trade with the right store format, whether it be Zales, Ratners or H Samuel, in the appropriate location.

The Group makes central decisions on ranges, shop fitting and space allocation within the stores to ensure a high degree of uniformity throughout each chain. The same item is displayed in virtually the same place in each window of a particular chain. To present each piece at its best we specify stringent lighting conditions, a set height and angle for the display pads and clear ticketing to describe the item and its price. Once the store is open sophisticated EPOS systems record each individual sale and trigger the replenishment cycle.

We spend considerable time and resources in recruiting and training our staff. As the competition for good quality staff increases we ensure that our staff are well paid and incentivised. Even temporary and part-time staff participate in sales bonus schemes.

Figure 25.5

Group strategic review: distribution

Jewellery retailing can be characterised as having a comparatively low average stockturn, with now a relatively low item value and a surge in sales at Christmas, the seasonal peak. Ratners' distribution systems have been developed in response to these challenges.

We have engineered a replenishment cycle which maximises in-stock positions in stores whilst minimising stockholding costs. It anticipates the peaks in seasonal demand before they happen and ensures that stores are fully stocked in readiness. It is also flexible enough to enable us to replenish stores in less than 24 hours during the crucial Christmas trading period. Our systems are so well developed that we have been described as 'retail engineers' by a team of leading retail analysts. The heart of the system is sophisticated EPOS. Terminals in every store are polled each night by a central computer. Zales/Ernest Jones' and Ratners' central computer and distribution systems are located in Colindale, North London, whilst H Samuel's systems are located in Birmingham. These computers send printed picking lists to the warehouses which forward the stock to the stores. The computers then model future demand on the basis of new sales data which is used to brief the supplier on required volume. As we refine this system further we are reducing the stock held in our stores and warehouses and calling stock off the suppliers at the last moment. This 'just-in-time' replenishment gives considerable savings to the Group by reducing costly stock levels.

In the US the same principles apply even though the distances involved are greater. Couriers take higher value stock from our head office in Akron, Ohio to stores two or three times a week. The frequency is increased during peak selling seasons such as Christmas. The closure of all distribution systems in the store chains we have acquired in the US and their consolidation into one central facility in Akron has led to large cost savings.

In 1989, 36,466,508 pieces of jewellery were despatched from our Group warehouses

Figure 25.6

Ratners' growth adds gloss to stores sector

by Terence Wilkinson, Assistant City Editor

RATNERS GROUP, the world's largest jewellers, brightened up the stores sector yesterday with the news that underlying sales growth in its core high street shops had accelerated to 24 per cent during the crucial December trading month.

Before December Ratners had been showing healthy sales growth on a store for store basis of about 18 per cent but Christmas trading stepped up the pace.

'We kept piling in the stock right up to Christmas Eve. It was a peak day and H Samuel, for instance, turned in sales of £12.5m compared with £8m last year – the shops were absolutely heaving', said Gerald Ratner, chairman of Ratners.

Sales made during December normally account for about 70 per cent of Ratners' annual turnover, which, coupled with the indication that the group had shrugged off the effects of a subdued background for consumer spending, led up to a 5p rise in Ratners shares to 268p.

'We took the view that it would be a tough Christmas for retailers and stepped up our seasonal advertising and incentives like a £50 gift voucher for purchases of over £150. Our suppliers paid for the advertising and the gift vouchers did not cost as much in the end so margins continued to rise,' said Mr Ratner.

Buying power and innovations such as hollow bracelets have enabled Ratners to lower the average selling price of its products from £19 to £15 over the year.

The best selling lines this Christmas were in the £10 range although gift sets of a bracelet, ear-rings and necklace at £29.95 did notably well.

News of buoyant sales at Ratners also produced sympathetic rises in high street retailers such as WH Smith which rose 7p to 353p and Marks and Spencer up 4p to 204½p.

For the first time Ratners gave a breakdown of sales growth in its constituent stores during December quoting figures on both a gross basis and on a like-for-like basis which excludes the effect of additional trading space.

On a gross and like-for-like basis sales at H Samuel rose by 28 per cent (22 per cent), Ratners by 32 per cent (24 per cent), Zales by 31 per cent (27 per cent), Watches of Switzerland by 16 per cent (11 per cent), Salisburys by 20 per cent (20 per cent) and Sterling in the US by 21 per cent (9 per cent).

(Independent, 3 Jan. 1990)

Figure 25.7

Late sales burst gives lift to Ratners and Boots

By Richard Bridges

RATNERS and Boots have confounded fears of poor Christmas trading with startling figures for the last week of seasonal shopping.

Gerald Ratner, chairman of the jewellery chain, reported group-wide increases for December and said sales in the last week before Christmas reached £100m in Britain alone. Boots meanwhile reported a 15 p.c. increase in the last week's trading at its Boots the Chemist chain, to £130m.

Ratners spent £6m on television advertising, gift vouchers and leaflets. Staff were awarded incentives, with stores staying open as late as midnight. 'If there was anyone about with money, we were open. We decided to throw the kitchen sink at it,' said Mr Ratner.

Both businesses reported strong sales of lower-priced items. The average sale price at Ratners fell from £18 to £14, and "millions" of the company's now famous 99p gold ear-rings were sold. 'The beginning of the month was not terrific but as we got closer to the day we put on phenomenal increases of 40 p.c. to 50 p.c.,' said Mr Ratner.

Among the group's subsidiary chains, Ratners and Zales produced like-for-like increases of 22 p.c. and 27 p.c. in December, with H Samuel increasing sales by almost a quarter.

Even Watches of Switzerland, where the average sale is £1,000, saw sales rise by 11 p.c. For December as a whole, Ratners took a total of £290m, against sales for the whole of the previous year of £635m.

In America, which is increasingly important to Ratners, cold weather meant that sales were no more than on target, with sales increases of 9 p.c. before new openings at the Sterling chain.

(*Independent*, 3 Jan. 1990)

Figure 25.8

Ratners' voucher success

By Gillian Bowditch

H SAMUEL, the Ratners subsidiary which distributed 102,000 £50 vouchers to customers who spent more than £150 just before Christmas, has had almost 60 per cent of them redeemed since the redemption period began in February.

The vouchers are valid until October, a traditionally quieter period for the jewellery business.

Mr Gerald Ratner, chairman and chief executive, says the discount offered is, in fact, nearer 10 per cent than 33 per cent as the average transaction for which the vouchers qualified was £200. The average purchase with a voucher is £70 and he believes that about 20 per cent of them will not be redeemed.

Ratners, whose new finance director, Mr Gary O'Brien, starts today, will announce final results on April 26.

Analysts are looking for pre-tax profits for the year of about £108 million, plus property profits of roughly £13 million, against £81 million last time.

(*Times*, 2 Apr. 1990)

Figure 25.9

Five year financial summary

(£000, except per share data)	1986	1987 *43 weeks*	1988	1989	1990 *53 weeks*
Sales	*44,840*	*158,178*	*360,205*	*635,160*	898,102
Profit on ordinary activities before taxation	*4,459*	*22,674*	*52,742*	*86,010*	121,488
Tax on profit on ordinary activities	*(1,352)*	*(8,493)*	*(20,833)*	*(31,824)*	(42,522)
Profit attributable to shareholders	*2,667*	*13,613*	*29,120*	*54,186*	79,060
Fully diluted earnings per 10p ordinary share*	*7.9p*	*14.7p*	*21.1p*	*26.5p*	30.2p
Ordinary dividends payable	*1,048*	*3,576*	*8,008*	*14,862*	20,098
Ordinary dividends per share (net)	*3.0p*	*4.0p*	*5.0p*	*7.5p*	9.5p
Capital expenditure	*3,105*	*10,747*	*49,517*	*52,143*	63,281
Depreciation	*1,361*	*3,899*	*8,871*	*16,536*	23,060
Net assets	*14,178*	*95,813*	*163,508*	*184,635*	297,900

* As adjusted for the rights issues in 1986, 1987 and 1988.

Figures 25.1, 25.2, 25.3, 25.4, 25.5, 25.9 reproduced with grateful thanks to Ratners Group PLC.

INVESTIGATION OF BUSINESS TERMS

Market segment. That part of the market at which the product is aimed in terms of the socio-economic groups and other characteristics that make them potential customers.

EPOS. This refers to the electronic point-of-sale system whereby the sales register is in effect a terminal linked to a main computer. Each terminal collects information on what and how much is being sold and passes this to the main computer. This then adjusts the stockholding figures for each retail outlet and issues orders to its own warehouses or suppliers to make the necessary deliveries.

Targeted gross margin. The profit margin that the company is seeking to achieve when comparing price paid to the suppliers and the price received by the retailers.

Customer traffic. The rate of flow of people past a retail outlet.

Estates and operations department. That part of the business which deals with the appraisal and acquisition of properties and their redevelopment as new retail outlets within an appropriate chain.

Average stockturn. Often referred to as 'rate of stockturn' or 'stock turnover rate'. This is the number of times during a specific period (frequently one year) that the average stockholding is being sold and replaced. Used as a measure of efficiency but with caution since a fast stockturn rate may indicate too low a price.

In-stock positions. Refers to the state of stock of specified items in the various retail outlets.

Picking list. Simply a document detailing the quantities, location and nature of the various items required to fulfil orders. Frequently computer-generated and nowadays often fed directly into automated 'picking' equipment such as fork-lift trucks, cranes and other devices which then obey the list and operate automatically to 'pick' the required items from shelves and deliver them to the assembly point.

Just-in-time. A system of provisioning (supplying an organization) which aims to reduce the waste associated with holding stocks. The theoretical ideal is to provide input at exactly the same rate as sales are being made. This is difficult to achieve, particularly in retailing, but can release working capital for more profitable use elsewhere.

SHORT-ANSWER QUESTIONS

1. Why is the sales growth in different parts of the Ratners Group measured on a like-for-like basis?
2. In the light of an inflation rate of 9.4 per cent in May 1990 comment on the performance of the Group's ordinary shares.
3. Explain how the changes made to the Salisbury shops are expected to improve their performance.
4. Why has Ratners' size and the use of computer technology helped its purchasing strategy?
5. Why do Ratners ensure a high degree of uniformity throughout each chain with respect to ranges, shopfitting, display, lighting and space allocation?
6. Why would a person who purchased Ratners' ordinary shares in 1986 earn a larger percentage dividend in 1990 than someone who bought them in 1989?
7. What kinds of spending by the Ratners Group would be classified as capital expenditure?

ANALYSING BUSINESS SITUATIONS

1. The Ratners Group claims that the rapid growth in the jewellery market has been due mainly to its own retailing methods. In the light of this statement:
   (a) explain the possible links between Ratners' retailing methods and the growth in the jewellery market;
   (b) other developments which may have contributed to growth in jewellery sales.
2. Between 1987 and 1990 interest rates doubled. This had a particularly severe effect on mortgage repayment and many high-street chains suffered as a result. What factor allowed Ratners to outperform its profit target over this period?
3. What factors may have led Ratners to move into the US market?
4. Describe some of the business and financial problems that might have arisen prior to Ratners' introduction of the 'just-in-time' stock replenishment cycle.
5. Comment on the relationships between the following, and account for any major changes:
   (a) sales and profits on ordinary activities before taxation;
   (b) gross profits and tax paid;
   (c) capital expenditure and depreciation;
   (d) capital expenditure and sales.

MFI

Figure 26.1

MFI – Development and Changes

MFI Furniture Centres have a strong position in the UK Market for bedroom, kitchen, lounge, and dining-room furniture. They are also involved in lighting, and textiles.

The MFI Company was started in 1964 by two enterprising small businessmen, who founded Mullard Furniture Industries, soon to become known as MFI. Originally this was a mail order business and traded in low-cost, self-assembly, flatpack furniture as well as a range of leisure products.

By 1969 MFI had opened up nine of its own retail stores in the London area. Three years later its operation had grown to 25 sites, where warehouses were used to display the assembled furniture alongside the flatpacks which were then sold on a cash-and-carry basis. These were out-of-town sites away from the crowded high streets. This was because MFI realized that the public needed to be able to pick up their goods in their cars. These sites also had the advantage of enough space to carry large stocks of flatpack items and to display an increasingly wider product range.

In 1974 MFI opened up its first purpose-built distribution centre at Bedford. This meant that the company could buy in bulk and suppliers could deliver to one location. Further economies of scale came from using its own transport fleet to deliver full loads to its warehouses. By 1975 it had 33 locations and had moved out of the mail order business.

As public tastes changed in the mid-1970s so MFI had to respond to changes in tastes and preferences. It abandoned the stacks of racked and palleted goods surrounding a single item of furniture and moved into 'room sets' and warehouse/pick-up points. Soon each store used showrooms and a large warehouse area for immediate pick-up close to ample, free parking facilities.

As the stores evolved, so did the range of products that they offered. Although MFI still emphasized value for money this was supported by a greater stress on quality and design. This reflected MFI's strategy to move 'up-market' as household disposable incomes increased. MFI had now reached the stage where it could take most, if not all, of its suppliers' output, and could therefore influence the design and construction methods of their products. To reflect these changes, MFI altered its name to MFI Furniture Centres.

The rate at which it expanded onto new sites led the Company to create MFI Properties Ltd. This vertical integration allowed it to deal directly with all property matters in both seeking and using new sites.

In 1980 its warehousing and distribution activities were expanded with the development and opening of a new national distribution centre at Northampton. This aspect of MFI's integration was now carried out on a 42-acre site with a covered storage area of one million square feet.

In the same year, MFI engaged in horizontal integration when it acquired Status Discount Ltd, a flat-pack furniture retailer concentrating mainly on kitchen and bedroom products on 66 locations, mainly in the northern part of the country.

Figure 26.2

In 1982 its marketing strategy led to the introduction of products carrying the Hygena brand name. As Hygena developed into a major supplier of kitchen and bedroom units MFI bought up the company in 1987.

A further major development in the marketing strategy in 1988 involved the purchase of Schreiber Furniture whose brand name was well known in the fitted kitchens and bedrooms market. This also gave MFI a strong foothold in the high street because Schreiber had a network of 115 independently owned dealerships and six company-owned stores. Hygena Kitchens were also launched in 45 W. H. Smith Do It All stores throughout the UK and Schreiber Kitchens and Bedrooms were introduced into 20 Sainsbury Homebase stores. The MFI Group further reinforced its position in the furniture manufacturing sector when it purchased Greens, a major manufacturer of components to the furniture industry. As a result the MFI group became even more highly integrated, with control over the full manufacturing process from the initial input of raw wood and chipboard to the output of finished furniture and its sale and installation.

By 1989 MFI had taken its total of furniture centres to over 140 and the group had a turnover of just over £600 million.

The Determinants of the Demand for MFI Products

Over a period of time there can be quite significant changes in the ways in which people spend their money. This is because of events and developments that influence the kinds of goods available, people's ability to buy these goods, and their willingness to do so. It is possible to identify the factors that influence the total demand for the kinds of products produced and sold by the MFI group.

1. Income – what people buy in the way of MFI products, and how much, is obviously determined by their income after deductions for tax and national insurance (disposable income). But a rise in disposable income will not necessarily allow a person to buy more goods and services if the rise in income is more than outweighed by the increase in the general level of prices (inflation).
2. Credit facilities – people's spending power is also determined by the amount of money they are able and willing to borrow. This may be in the form of loans from banks and building societies; use of credit cards, including those issued by stores; and goods obtained on hire purchase agreements. The total demand for the kinds of goods normally bought on credit may also be affected by significant changes in interest charges on credit. MFI obviously benefits when credit is cheap and plentiful because this is when a lot of money will be spent.
3. Tastes and preferences – these are largely determined by advertising and the extent to which MFI is successful in getting information about its products across to potential customers and highlighting selling points, which will result in increased sales.
4. Competition from other goods and services outside the furniture industry – the demand for furniture could be influenced by other things such as changes in the price of foreign holidays, home entertainment centres and cars.
5. Goods and services that are generally bought together – in many cases the purchase of furnishings will be connected with people moving home. Therefore the market demand for furniture will be directly influenced by the mortgage rate and house prices.
6. Demographic and social change – over a period of time the pattern of demand will switch in favour of furniture due to the following factors:
   (a) an increase in the number of people in the age group when they started to set up home together;
   (b) how the population is spread between cities, towns, suburban areas and the countryside;
   (c) an increase in the number of dual income households will create a demand for labour saving and convenient room designs and furniture. More importantly the larger total household income will provide the means of financing these improvements.

Figures 26.1 and 26.2 adapted from MFI *Take a Look at Us Now*.

Figure 26.3

Government Economic Policy and its Effects on the Market for Furniture

Manufacturers and retailers of consumer durables such as furniture tend to feel the first impact of measures introduced by the government to tackle inflation and combat problems associated with the balance of trade. Anti-inflation policies are aimed at deflating the total level of demand in the economy to a point where it can be satisfied by output without inflationary pressures arising in the labour market. Total household expenditure, for example, may be curbed by some of the following measures:

(a) A rise in interest rates will make it more expensive to buy on credit. High interest will also increase household's mortgage repayments, which means that less money will be available to buy consumer durable goods such as furniture and to meet repayments on any new credit.
(b) Making credit less attractive by stipulating a minimal deposit and repayment period, which will obviously hit furniture sales.
(c) A restriction on the growth of loans and overdrafts from banks and other financial institutions.
(d) An increase in income tax and rates which will reduce the level of household disposable incomes.
(e) An increase in personal allowances which does not reach the rate of inflation, thus reducing the real purchasing power of this part of tax free income.
(f) A rise in the general level of VAT which means that households' incomes will not go as far as before and some items will have to be given up.
(g) A higher rate of VAT on those items which can be used as a particularly effective way of reducing people's spending power.

The measures listed above will create a business environment whereby businesses, including those in the furniture industry, will reduce the demand for labour and stand firm against excessive pay demands. Deflated markets mean that such businesses must pay more attention to their costs and be more competitive if they are to survive.

The business will also be directly influenced by the government's anti-inflation policy, because the cost of borrowing will rise and unfortunately this may cause the business to shelve or cut its investment programmes. Higher borrowing costs may also force the business to look more closely at its labour costs in order to reduce the level of its borrowing. This is another reason why businesses avoid big pay increases and it encourages them to become more competitive.

A combination of inflation and too much spending in the economy may produce a trade deficit. Anti-inflationary measures and the deflation of demand will eventually help to close the trade gap; but the government may still feel that it is necessary to bring about a fall in the exchange rate. Although this will help UK exporters to be more competitive abroad, it is not good news for firms such as MFI which manufacture and sell products which use some imported components and materials. One advantage for MFI is that retailers who have relied upon selling imported furniture will face higher prices.

ANALYSING BUSINESS SITUATIONS

1. You are employed as a market research assistant with MFI. It is part of the company's on-going strategy to identify market opportunities where MFI can readily expand its activities. In particular, your department has been asked to look into the possibility of increasing its involvement in the following:

(a) office type furniture;
(b) conservatory and patio furniture.

The head of your section has been asked to attend a meeting of the marketing department to appraise current and future market opportunities. In preparation for this meeting, she asks you to provide her with briefing notes. These should cover the following:

(a) information and data relating to demand factors;
(b) recent and anticipated future developments in government economic policy and the possible impact upon market demand.

2. You hold a position in the Internal Administration and Planning Department of MFI. If the company was to expand its interests in the two markets described in (1) it might buy out an existing manufacturer of each product. It has considered a German manufacturer of the office-type furniture located near to Frankfurt and trading under the name Beckenbauer. At the same time, MFI have shown an interest in purchasing Suntrap Furniture, located in Kent and specializing in conservatory and patio furniture. You are asked to prepare an internal memorandum, which identifies the advantages and disadvantages to MFI of these possible takeovers. This memorandum is to be circulated to the marketing, design, purchasing, personnel and finance departments at the head office and to the production managers at the factories already owned by MFI. The memorandum should stress how MFI has benefited in the past from expansion through integration.